Visits and Other Passages

by

Carol Smallwood

Finishing Line Press
Georgetown, Kentucky

Visits and Other Passages

Publisher: Leah Maines

Editor: Christen Kincaid

Cover Art: Vera Gubnitskaia - http://vera-gubnitskaia-art.blogspot.com/

Author Photo: Cheboygan Daily Tribune

Cover Design: Leah Huete

Printed in the USA on acid-free paper.
Order online: www.finishinglinepress.com
                also available on amazon.com

Author inquiries and mail orders:
Finishing Line Press
P. O. Box 1626
Georgetown, Kentucky 40324
U. S. A.

Table of Contents

Part III Capturing Words

Part IV Conjectures

Epilogue: Passage

Foreword

A picture may paint a thousand words, but Carol Smallwood's words paint a million images and all museum worthy. *Visits and Other Passages* is a travel narrative. But the journey is not one of general sightseeing. Instead, through a collection of her poetry, vignettes and essays the reader is taken on a tour of both Smallwood's personal inner life and potent thoughts and ideas. Whether discussing location and character or the lady at Wendy's, Smallwood presents truths comfortingly familiar, fascinatingly foreign, and intellectually thought provoking. This is the stuff of the best excursions.

Present in this work are the range of experiences and emotions present in a life lived. Through detail and humor, we see ourselves, our neighbors, and the characters we know of in stories. We also learn of old books, science, and novelist. In "Library Passages" Smallwood asks, "who will be the custodians of culture? What is worth preserving?" interesting questions in the context of this journey.

Perhaps unwittingly, I suggest Smallwood answers these important questions within the pages of this work. We are all the custodians of culture, whither we are novelist or Avon lady, for the importance of culture lay in our memories, our experiences, our relationship with the world and others. All things are worth preserving, as it is all things that not only make us who we are, but more importantly connect us to each other.

Su Epstein, Ph.D., Library Director, Saxton B. Little Free Library, Columbia, Connecticut: librarianship reviewer, researcher, and writer with a MA in Sociology.

Introduction

Visits and Other Passages is a novella length mix of short stories, vignettes, expository essays, letters, lyrical essays, flash fiction, free verse poems, formal poems, on the topic of visits and passages. Various genre were used in the hopes of grasping the subtle aspects and shades inherent in the wide range of visits and passages one experiences—as in most things relating to humans, they are neither simple or straight forward. The words of Heracleitus: "We are estranged from that with which we are most familiar" still rings true.

The collection is divided into: Part I: The Hearth; Part II: Slants and Other Perspectives; Part III: Capturing Words; Part IV: Conjectures.

For readers curious about formal poems I've included types and examples in the collection: Sonnet—Choice of Navigators; Pantoum—Sewing by Day; Villanelle—A Hardcover Book; Triolet—To Wonder; Tercet—Leo; Cinquain—Prufrock Napkins; Rondeau—An Unlikely Introduction.

My thanks to Dr. Su Epstein for the foreword; the blurb writers: Chris Swanberg, Mary Barnet, Katherine Mayfield, Sarah Cisse, Dr. Mary Langer Thompson, and Dr. Christine Redman-Waldeyer.

Carol Smallwood

Prologue

One December Day

a fly walked slowly across my
computer screen like it was cold
but knew it was colder outside—
and it was waiting too

A magnifying glass showed
more than I cared as it nibbled
fruitcake with an occasional
flick of leg

Part I

The Hearth

A Visit from Caesar's Wife

In the spring I located an Avon Lady to help make me feel more at home.

"Do you know you have a wasp's nest out there?" the Avon Lady asked scurrying inside. When I'd called, she mentioned her grandson and how many years she'd been an Avon representative, so I figured she'd be about my age and looked forward to seeing her.

"Oh, is that right? My goodness!" But I didn't mind it by the doorbell because it kept solicitors away.

The Avon Lady, in a pink dress, had a cap of close fitting dark hair that looked just like the wig called "Caesar's Wife" in a catalog I'd received. My visitor wore perfectly applied matching dusty rose lipstick and nail polish. In Nicolet City, the most visible member of the country club was a handshaking insurance agent with his well-dressed wife at his side in high heels with matching lipstick and nail polish.

She said, "I know it's late for a calendar, but aren't they delightful? This year they did them in such delightful pastels and I like them so much better than brash colors. I always wished I'd had a girl to dress in pink." When she pointed to the pink skeins of yarn piled in a basket with some kittens for the month of February, I noticed she had whiskers like the woman in Nicolet City who'd quivered for bits of gossip—the Avon Lady's round bright eyes were like hers too.

I thanked her for the calendar and took the stapled bag holding my order she presented like crown jewels. Smiling, I said, "Please have a seat." When I returned to the living room with my credit card I told her, "I try and put as much on the card as I can because the Doris Day Animal League gets a percentage of it," hoping she'd might be interested in getting one.

"Oh, yes. I use mine to get frequent flyer miles to visit my other son. I see him so often you know."

When she was filling out credit card information, I asked, "Is it hot in town too?"

The way she said, "Well, I think you have more of a breeze here," I knew she'd gotten a good whiff of the neighbor's cow manure. Caesar's Wife sat very straight, her small feet precisely together. Her high black pointed shoes were like the kind that were buttoned with a button hook in earlier times; she sat with her back not touching the couch like a proper lady doing a needlepoint sampler. When handing my Visa receipt she said, "It's been warm going to my grandson's baseball games. He's nine years old and looks just like my son at that age." She glanced around before putting her copy of the order in her purse and said, "I'm sorry your order's a bit late, but my husband and I are going on vacation and I've had so much to do you know."

I could tell she was trying to figure out where I fit in the scheme of things, just like I pegged her kitchen as one with a teddy bear cookie jar on a spotless white counter always cleaned with antibacterial wipes—the kind advertised as killing 99.9% of bacteria. She probably had pastel Pennsylvania Dutch paper toweling, doormats with pastel teddy bears for her grandchildren, and proper eyelet (white) tieback curtains. Yes, Caesar's wife "must be above suspicion."

"I'm so glad to have found an Avon lady again. I've used Avon for over thirty years where I lived before."

"Where was that?"

"In Nicolet City."

When she tilted to one side and asked, "Why did you ever come here?" I tried to tell if her hair was really a wig, but just the curls on her forehead moved—curls like the picture in Jenny's book on nursery rhymes about the girl with the curl in the middle of her forehead.

"Oh, I wanted to take classes. I guess I wasn't finished with school." Yes, I believed in reason and enjoyed the smell of it in rectangular classrooms with rows of desks facing a larger desk. A projection screen with a string, that, when partially down, reminded me of Kitty forgetting to pull her tongue back in. You could tell a lot about a teacher by how they dealt with the string dangling in the middle of the blackboard. Classrooms had blackboards with smudged words much more intriguing because of their vagueness—whole banks of fluffy erasures with tails of "Y's" and "J's" still showing. I remember reading that if someone from the 1800's walked into a classroom they'd feel right at home because classrooms had changed so little.

I recalled another kind of school—a homemaker's school in Nicolet City where you could select: how to grow mung beans, how to make curtains from percale sheets, how to make your own baby food out of green beans. Mark had been in school and Jenny stayed with other kids in a room with some 4-H girls. After a cafeteria lunch, I saw a film on how Lee's carpets were made and a demonstration on cleaning Sears ovens. I returned loaded with Wisconsin Consolidated Gas recipes on cards; each card had a blue tear-shaped flame of gas in the upper left corner.

"Why, you sound like my sister who doesn't know what she wants.

She's an ex-ray technician and wants to change jobs at forty-five." Caesar's Wife shook her head, "Still doesn't know her place. Single, too," her eyes trailing to my left hand. And as if she still couldn't pigeonhole me, asked, "You work?"

"I retired after twenty years from Parisburg Public Schools."

"Oh." She looked a bit surprised but lost no time in replying, "You probably never had much time to bake cookies did you? My sons loved oatmeal cookies like my grandson does, you know. I make them with coconut, raisins, and walnuts," and proceeded to give me the recipe.

When I'd ordered men's talc and after-shave on the phone a few weeks ago, she'd said, "It sounds like you know what someone likes," but I hadn't replied. When I examined the Friktion and Uomo talcs now, I almost said they were for myself to see her expression. Truth was, they were. I liked the solidity, the calming masculinity. Especially the citrus tones because they reminded me of the men I liked remembering.

I'd have to see if Honeysuckle was in the new catalog. I wanted to order it even after telling myself I was wallowing where I shouldn't. Ah, there was nothing like the pale cloying sweetness of Honeysuckle! When I needed to remember what being in love was like, Honeysuckle brought a hint of the perpetual spring back. I recognized the look in the Avon model dipping her hand in a stream floating with daisies: she was smiling—no, glowing with anticipation in her eyes and sunlight on her hair: "Every moment's to be lived. Your rush to greet the dawn…and love." And to live the moment you just had to rub your wrist on the sample. You didn't even have to unfold samples anymore. The next page showed a model wearing a night gown (I think) with rose petals falling on her matching those on the gown of the Avon Lady's nail and lipstick shade—Love's Promise.

It was funny though, what I bought looked smaller than it did in the catalog; the shower gels that hooked on the shower weren't really much bigger than tubes of toothpaste. And Avon was selling so many other things now like cell phones. But it was reassuring once again to have an Avon catalog even it they were so much thicker now. Size 6 models still had tangles of curly hair, perfect teeth, matching lipstick and nails, and trailed pale pink scarves on pale pink beaches. Toddler models with chubby legs held peaches in pink baskets. I saw a woman walking into a fluffy lake with upraised arms with her hair blowing one way and her gown the other, featuring the new fragrance, Perception.

Still, I'd look at the next catalog that the Avon Lady said she'd hang it on my door knob if I wasn't home and give the bag an extra twist so the wind wouldn't carry it off. Avon made me feel a part of things: it was as American as McDonald's, the Fourth of July, or the *Reader's Digest*.

When debating what to do with the calendar, I wondered if the photographer had used a pink screen over the lens or if the muted look was part of the developing. The look was warm, romantic, real and yet just out of reach—and I understood why the Avon Lady had said: "Women like the pastel look. It's such a delight. So feminine and flattering, you know."

Beginning the Day

Dawn, invading the room—a small bedroom that didn't yet reveal its corners—moved with the inexorable passage of time as it was in so many other rooms revealing subtleties when it was ready. The room—an ordinary one in the Midwest was built with an eye for cost cutting and boasted a walk in closet and large alcove between the window and the door filled with shelves. Vague forms hinted where the shelves were on the expanse of white wall as light advanced with its imperceptible speed.

The historian could have easily detected clues about the rise of the human species from the type of shelter and how adequately it advanced it since cave man days; the sociologist could have written much on the affect of living in such a house had for man as a social animal and the development of the family; an architect, the progress and popularity of low to the ground ranch homes in the United States no matter the region and for all incomes. The ranch house is attributed to being American in origin—the one story floor plan with attached garage and shutters can be seen about anywhere. The landscape it was on did much to make it look different.

Critical day slipped through the blinds and disclosed shelves on the south wall: a pedestal dish with artificial drooping green and purple grapes; clock set a few minutes early; high school graduation picture of an oldest grandchild and her brother; Galsworthy's books; sprig of wild strawberries always perky green and red; paper roses in paper vase on gossamer hairpin lace; photos of Kitty all amber eyes, Minnie with Christmas bow; pottery repaired so the crack was almost invisible. The CD's: Sean Connery and Alec Baldwin in *Hunt for Red October*; a young Hugh Laurie as Bertie Wooster before *House, M.D.*; Pavarotti's *La Boheme*.

A rectangle was becoming discernable on the wall: from its approximate location and shape Lily knew it was a painting so familiar it was impossible to describe—one found as the backing of another picture. It hung by the door taking form.

The shelves on the west wall held things mostly forgotten but taking anything away would be removing a thread capable of unraveling the whole such as: bronzed baby shoes; a bread wrapper holding stones from Lily's grandfather's land secured by ribbon; a telephone directory from a country she'd never been; an old *The United States Government Manual* that organized a maze; *The Adventures of Sherlock Holmes* with tales that never failed to bring her into another time and place as new Sherlock's on screen changed; a picture of an aunt who read *The Wind in the Willows* with so much enjoyment when she was small she concluded printed words were special; a photo from a magazine of "The Thinker"; *The Far Side Gallery 4*; her childhood globe that had the loyalty to stay the same in a changing world; a wicker basket of large cloth red roses recently washed with a hope it wouldn't destroy them; a picture of grandchildren taken when they seemed so grown up but now seemed the children they really were; the red dish cloth knitted by a cousin in such a beautiful red under a b/w photo of her grandfather who always stood very straight.

The shelves revealed more in the increasing impersonal light; cancelled stamps waiting to join others in a large pickle jar; drapery rings from drapes no longer up; a miniature doll always standing with a plume in her hair. And finally the light showed possible dust but one doesn't see dust unless up close in full daylight on book shelves.

The carpet was gray which encouraged what furniture was beginning to take shape appear it was floating, reminding Lily of a scene long ago of cattle near a woods with just their heads visible in the fog. Hearing cowbells helped convince her the scene was real and not imaginary—since she's often thought that the strangest thing of all was not to see how strange things really were.

Dreams usually retreated like fog and there was no retrieving them if you didn't write down a few key words to bring them back. The subconscious is a labyrinth only for the brave or those who've no other choice but to face things: those who've concluded that whatever was lurking couldn't be more destructive than what was being lived—in other words, who've reached the end of the line. Lily was used to hearing the gate clang shut that blocked recalling dreams.

Lily's blinds saw the unrelenting dawn through slats: they allowed more control, and she'd never regretted the investment. Closing one's eyes, making believe it is still night sometimes worked for falling back asleep.

A land study of Freedom County had been made by the United States Department of Agriculture's Soil Conservation Service in a publication of many pages with a cover of an air view of the typical countryside. Lily got a copy when she moved and it was filled with terms like: permeability, moraine, till plains, glaciofluvial deposits. She copied the land description on her land title, then followed the 6 steps to find her specific land using the large fold out maps and tables but gave up before learning it. The lengthy fieldwork publication was good to have and one day she'd figure out what kind of land she was on and how it came to be—the research in the heavy book was to be much admired.

Minnie, waiting outside the closed door, walked in with her tail up. When asked, "How are you this morning? Have you been a good girl?" the tail went even straighter while making her usual rounds. She always expected to find something under the dresser that had a scarf with a note pinned under: "Made by Grandma Persea from a flour sack"; if Minnie found a pen she'd roll it so Lily could see it and then flop on her side to be petted. The cat would fetch plastic cups that came with bottles of upset stomach medicine when tossed; her other cats had not fetched like this. Over and over again, she'd jump in the air trying to catch the small cup before it fell and then proudly carry it in her mouth to Lily to have it thrown again. She had been called Minnie at the animal shelter because she was small.

The dresser had a mirror with streaks showing its age. If the angle was changed it was disconcerting so Lily was careful not to touch it. The thick white fringed drawn work scarf had traces of black lettering of a flour company and was Lily's favorite because it reminded her of her grandmother making the best with what she had: the delicate lace she made when threads were pulled somehow gave Lily reassurance.

Near the dresser, two white plaster acanthus leaf pedestals held a shelf with bottles of Estée Lauder to admire and a box wrapped at the mall with a self-addressed label: "To the Woman of the House"—what was inside forgotten. On the box a bug that looked like a lady bug was deciding which direction to go. It was always a guessing game of when to put bugs outside as even though it was almost April it could still snow. Yesterday a fly in the living room looked like it was waking up.

Dawn is a time when one is not sure what was real as you fought the pull of a dream that didn't make any sense but was comforting: when opening your eyes, the lingering shadows made you search desperately for anything to cling to like a survivor off the *Titanic*.

The light from the modem on the desk was becoming less noticeable now the room was getting lighter. Light was revealing the miniature mirrors topped with gilt bows—reproductions of Victorian mirrors from an era held now to be hopelessly old fashioned. When the computer keyboard took form, Lily got up and began the day.

A Return

When I returned home, I stopped the car in the drive. I'd spent more money on my new house than I'd planned but at least it was relatively new, one level, with no close neighbors, and a convenient distance from White Rapids. And paid for. I rested my eyes on a fluffy cloud above the house until it changed from a smoke belching train to a horse kicking up its heels. I tried to tell how the sun could shine on only one side of small trees but couldn't. A flock of birds settled in some trees for a moment, took off in a rounded group, separated, and began swooping up and down like stitching up the air with long loops of thread. How did they decide what direction to go? Did they have a leader or did they all know? I hadn't seen that kind of bird until I moved to White Rapids and I remembered a dream: "I was at Uncle Walt's and saw many stuffed birds. Their eyes moved. I asked if they could be still alive even if stuffed and was told yes. I felt awful and wanted to help them escape but how could they live?"

I saw something brown on the ground and my heart started racing—but it was only a fallen branch and not a crouching stray cat. Then I remembered my last dream: "I was with relatives at Uncle Walt's and went for a walk. I listened to crickets, thinking the fields looked like quilts when I saw flames in the sky where Nicolet City was. I could see red flames shooting out over the trees and went back to tell them, terrified. Uncle Walt didn't want to hear of it and turned the baseball game on and the rest went along with him. He told me to put a belt on my skirt because it looked awful the way it was. I couldn't relax and went down the road and people were streaming out of town and I stopped a boy to ask where the fire was and he said it was downtown by the river near the oil storage tanks. When I got to the bridge it was all congested and I couldn't get across and wondered if fire reached me I could go into the river and if I'd die from the cold or from the heat.

I remembered that people had cooked in the water during the fires of 1878. I decided to walk back to Uncle Walt's and try to make them leave; when I went past a prehistoric dinosaur spot I saw a dinosaur and wondered if it'd be the only thing to survive. Then I thought I should get the car by the bridge to save time and turned back trying to run but it was too far and I was too tired. People were streaming out of town and the fire made it very light out. There were people at the bridge selling expensive rides to safety. I didn't know what to do—if I took the car my family would be stranded. When I woke up my eyes were watering as if from smoke and I had trouble swallowing, was stiff, afraid to move, felt hot from the flames, and still heard the roar of the fire.

I'd asked my Re/Max realtor (the one with the red, white, blue filled hot air balloon so full of possibilities) how White Rapids got its name. I expected a river with rapids but the land was flat without rivers or large trees; many large fields of corn were divided by straight roads punctuated by red stop signs every mile.

The trees in the woods in the back of my house were mostly small and slim because the ground was too wet to support large ones—if they got too tall or large, they toppled over taking a lot of ground and roots with them and the mounds added to the Devonian Era feeling. A feeling they were telling a tale I would never understand or believe; the lack of tall trees encouraged a wide expansive skyline that made me feel I had nowhere to hide. The expansive sky stared at me like an eye without eyelashes. I think Kitty felt this too because when she went out she'd carefully sniff in the doorway and once out, she'd walk near the house until she made a dash to a shrub offering cover.

Mounds Keep Appearing

on my lawn, except when covered with snow: a city from the
Mound Builder era. One wag frowns pronouncing gophers, one
swears it's moles offering methods of killing with wagging heads.

Rather than killing, I bought two sonic rockets, that once buried
were to chase the catacomb residents to large fields in all
directions.

"To chase away burrowing rodents, you have to think like one,"
the directions said. But, plagued by dreams of families
forsaking homes, the rockets were dug up, the batteries saved.

So, it is back to stepping around mounds, wondering what
subterranean life is listening under foot, and trying to see
designs in newly dug mounds.

No longer plagued by dreams of the underground homeless,
I read words on Vibrasonic Molechaser boxes:
"Don't let your molehills become mountains."

Wendy's

Signs in White Rapids are either small, nonexistent, or faded. Even the hospital has a barely noticeable sign like if you didn't know where it was you had no business going. When old cartographers drew maps having unknown areas, they named them in large letters, Unknown Terrors, Ultima Thule.

The organizations I attended when I first came to White Rapids were mostly run by the same people, mostly women. Most likely, in a college town, residents were used to students and professors coming and going, and decided it was safer to stick with the same people. After five years in White Rapids, I was just beginning to receive tentative headshakes by clerks in stores I frequented. When I went to the bank, I caught snatches on the red digital letters of newsline: Pittsburg Pirates 9 saves/opposing peace with Palestine/bases loaded in the ninth/killing of Saddam Hussein's sons/your bank has the best mortgage rates.

My car needed a 3,000-mile oil change and maintenance check so the service man met me at Wendy's and said, "It'll take about four hours because we can't do anything until the engine cools off." I hardly recognized him in his summer clothes—the last time I'd met him he was in winter ones and I'd read *Moby Dick* for class.

Four hours, good grief. But I didn't want to go to the service place because they had a dirty white kitten. There were more business types at Wendy's at noon. I sat at my usual table for two, arranged my meal on the table, put my earplugs in.

Wendy's wasn't as busy as I thought it'd be at noon. I read The *Canterbury Tales* over chili, a baked potato, and a senior Diet Pepsi. The routine was comforting: put butter and sour cream on the potato, put the lid on while I ate the chili. Only three hours to go. I could handle it. A woman shuffled. She saw. She conquered by smiling at a group of other scruffy women. They smiled. She belonged. I envied her. A Wendy's employee who'd always been friendly entered but she walked by without recognizing me.

Where could I go when I got my car? Maybe somewhere where I'd see tabloid headlines such as: "3500-Year-Old Mummy Gives Birth" and "Oprah Loses 63 Pounds to Marry Elvis"—they were more human and probably as relevant as regular newspaper headlines. The place mat showed a portion of a Big Bacon Classic Cheeseburger under a magnifying glass with a slice of red tomato kissed by condensation, lettuce, bacon, cheese, and hamburger. Things were as muffled as when I was a child swimming underwater in Lake Michigan.

A customer didn't go through the maze of railings but went directly to the counter. Then another did the same and others just kept falling in behind.

One of my writing professors said she wrote at the House of Pancakes while drinking black coffee and listening to loud music on her walkman and pictured her jerky, nervous movements. Had she ever thought about how many forms of tiny life had been in her coffee before it'd been brewed? After it was? Yes, earplugs were worth every penny—I could hardly hear some wailing baby—I started using them after hearing people discuss strays.

Another baby carried in one of those basket-like seats; pink feet twisting. At least she had a boy with her but saw no wedding rings—a couple for now. Still, couldn't wedding rings become nooses despite greeting cards proclaiming Love Is Eternal? Funny, despite the trend toward unisex clothes and unisex restrooms, girls displayed so much cleavage it was embarrassing. I tried to picture her a year from now, in ten.

A woman walked in wearing a baggy cardigan over a cotton dress. Her handbag (the kind Queen Elizabeth carried) was extended over her wrist as she made her way to the counter in sensible shoes. She took a long time counting her money and the cashier cupped her mouth to stifle a laugh.

One of the pictures on the wall was like one Monet would've done. Mitchell had taken me to an exhibition on impressionists when I'd gone to the University of Wisconsin—Ithaca; we'd liked Monet the best. Whenever I hear Chopin, I am in that place that is ours with no end or beginning.

When I went though the maze to get Crispy Chicken Nuggets, it was like some fashion runway after watching people coming and going so long. Once seated again, I partially removed my earplugs to hear the women behind me but the hum of the air conditioning and ice being scooped muffled things. One of the women kept laughing. All I was able to make out was "At least that's what I heard." When I got the Caesar Side Salad and more Diet Pepsi, the new placemat had puzzles to spot the robot unlike the other robots.

Another couple. The girl kept pulling down a skimpy spaghetti strap top not reaching her hip hugger jeans. A boy, matting his hair with nervous fingers making it look like Kitty's hairballs.

I wondered if they'd soon be like that young couple with kids at a back table—the floor was littered with straws, napkins, Wendy's suggestion cards, French fries, catsup—sort of a calling card of the young family. The girl, about seven, in chucky shoes, had used the rails leading to the counter like a ballet rail until spotting Clifford the Red Dog toys.

Things became hushed, transitional to dinner.

People wandered by not unlike the *Canterbury Tales* while the Beatles belted out, *I Want to Hold Your Hand*; people so alike and so unalike, so endlessly interesting. I kept straining to see some detail in them to define myself and once again wondered how people could become science fiction addicts when what's real is so fantastic. The natives of Alaska had so many names for snow because they observed their world; I'd lived long enough in Nicolet City to know that the different sounds of waves were more than I'd ever guess. In White Rapids, ordering the same thing was not unlike the variations of a theme in classical music: no two baked potatoes were the same.

A man blocked my view. The service man!

A man leaving the parking lot motioned me to walk by and I automatically switched on my a-man-is-around face, smiled and walked faster; he lowered the window of his pick-up grinning, adjusted his baseball cap, and said, "I believe in beauty before age."

When waiting at a stop light, a NPR announcer said that most musicals so popular during the Great Depression were lavish escapist productions because people didn't want to see what was going on. The stop light, one of those with green flashing arrows for turns, seemed a square dance caller guiding cars to take an Allemande Left or an Allemande Right on their promenade home. Do Sa Do Around the Left-Hand Lady and See Saw....

Stop lights in Nicolet City didn't have those flashing green arrows. I remember one snowy Christmas Eve coming home with the kids after Midnight Mass waiting for the one stop light in Nicolet City to change. The kids had laughed because we hadn't seen a car for miles; the red was the only color in our the black and white trip.

Grandmother Said

"You are never lonely if you have needle and thread."
She sat straight, wore her hair Gibson Girl style,
fashioned pillow cases with crocheted pink roses for her bed
and made log cabin quilts with invisible stitches by the mile.

She sat straight, wore her hair Gibson Girl style,
her dresser scarves were round, or more often, square
and made log cabin quilts with invisible stitches by the mile
while grandfather listened to baseball—they stayed a pair.

Her dresser scarves were round, or more often, square;
she designed soap holders the color of fall leaves:
while grandfather listened to baseball—they stayed a pair.
The pure linen she used in doilies is rare everyone believes.

She designed soap holders the color of fall leaves,
fashioned pillow cases with crocheted pink roses for her bed;
the pure linen she used in doilies is rare everyone believes.
"You are never lonely if you have needle and thread."

A Supermarket Triptych

Did the passersby think I was a restaurant owner instead of there
to enjoy the colossal bags and jars Alice in Wonderland size?
A Motown tune belted out love and emotions—places I didn't dare.
Did the passersby think I was a restaurant owner instead of there
to wonder, check the sales, notice anything new, leisurely stare
as I sip my courtesy cup of decaf, speculate on good looking guys?
Did the passersby think I was a restaurant owner instead of there
to enjoy the colossal bags and jars Alice in Wonderland size?

The middle of supermarket aisles are good as neither side receives
any preference as if Queen Elizabeth surveying waiting fans,
nodding to the Clabber Girl while sipping decaf, A.M. Reprieve.
The middle of supermarket aisles are good as neither side receives
a longer inspection than the other especially when one perceives
potato chips, chocolate on sale—best run to the aisle of pans.
The middle of supermarket aisles are good as neither side receives
any preference as if Queen Elizabeth surveying waiting fans.

The grocery bottles of extra virgin oil stood in extra straight lines
on top shelves, labels maroon or yellow—the white delightfully prim
covering their round fronts facing aisles as if fashion runway designs.
The grocery bottles of extra virgin oil stood in extra straight lines
exotic, sophisticated, as if competing with bottles of imported wines
so not to be neglected, sidelined—relegated to bottom shelf confines.
The grocery bottles of extra virgin oil stood in extra straight lines
on top shelves, labels maroon or yellow—the white delightfully prim.

Sewing by Day

A chair by a window is best for selecting pieces in quilt making:
light of day, natural light, best reveals shades, flaws in pieces
of boxes on boxes of clothes carefully cut—a slow undertaking;
quilt after quilt has made my children question output increases.

Light of day, natural light, best reveals shades, flaws in pieces.
"Who's your quilts for?" I'm asked as stacked quilts grow higher.
Quilt after quilt has made my children question output increases
and I picture the stacks after I'm gone going up in a night pyre.

"Who's your quilts for?" I'm asked as stacked quilts grow higher:
plaid, plain, striped, flowered, flannel, fleece, denim, cotton
and I picture the stacks after I'm gone going up in a night pyre—
memories stored in cut clothes and pieces not yet forgotten.

Plaid, plain, striped, flowered, flannel, fleece, denim, cotton
of boxes on boxes of clothes carefully cut—a slow undertaking:
memories stored in cut clothes and pieces not yet forgotten.
A chair by a window is best for selecting pieces in quilt making.

Polly's Visit

Polly arrived in her husband's pick-up. It was a stretch for her to get out because she was a little woman and I had to smile because a Ford pick-up didn't quite coincide with my image of a retired tiny registered nurse whose receding chin emphasized her bird-like look. Although I hadn't seen her since we were kids, her brown eyes were as full of life as ever even though her auburn hair had that out-of-a-bottle shade.

"Oh, I love your house," said Polly after hugs.

"Thanks!" I hung her coat up and asked, "Did you have any trouble finding my place?"

"No, none at all. Your directions were super clear." Her voice had such a ring of unbounded optimism I felt like extending my foot so she'd fall on her beak-like nose. Polly put her hands on her hips and twisted to one side until her bones "were heard from" and then did the same to the other side. She used to pop her knuckles so I checked to see if they were oversized like Aunt Hester said they'd be and when I saw they weren't I felt disappointed and cheated.

"I'll put your boots on the furnace to dry."

"Oh, that'd be super."

"Please have a seat." I left her patting her hair perched on the edge of the chair. When I returned from the utility room I said, "You're very brave to drive from St. Paul this time of the year."

Polly dismissed it with a wave of her hand and said, "Oh, I asked St. Christopher to keep his eye on me." She added with such conviction, "I have a super guardian angel," that I glanced above her shoulder half expecting to see an angel as portrayed on holy cards awarded to good children at St. John's Catholic School—in a white robe, barefooted in midair, smiling, with perky wings. Polly looked at me carefully and said, "You look well in green. And how'd you do it—you don't have any lines on your face."

I looked down at my green jumper and said, "Oh, thanks." I'd been told in high school home ec class when we'd taken turns holding color swatches against each other's throats, that green was my color because it highlighted my green eyes. Others had complimented my skin—but lately it'd been dubbed "youthful." My square chin had always contrasted with my fair skin, blonde hair, and even features—Polly's cheeks had a blotchy look some children have; her nose was still so pointed it didn't look real.

"Would you like some tea? I have some apple cinnamon, mint, or orange pekoe."

"Mint sounds super."

After I'd put the kettle on I said, "I'll give you a little tour of my house if you like" because she'd kept sitting on the edge of the chair like a bird anticipating a worm.

"I'd love one. You have a lot of privacy here, don't you?"

"It's almost too secluded but I wanted a quiet spot."

"You have quite a bit of room."

"No matter what you have I don't think you ever have enough closet or storage space and have come to the conclusion, if you have space, you'll fill it." When I came to the first room down the hall I said, "This is Scott's room."

"I see lots of blueprints. He's a contractor?"

When I replied, "Architect," I noted with satisfaction that Polly was impressed. "It's very hard for Jenny to be away from him. He got a phone for the room and uses a calling card—their monthly bill must be terrible. He describes every new house he looks at for them in great detail."

"It's super you have him around to help you settle in."

"Yes, he's been a great help. He's easy to have around." I waved my hand, "You can see he's pretty neat."

The next room was a storage room filled with things I couldn't part with—things I hoped someday the kids or their kids would treasure—I hadn't anything of my parent's except a quilt my mother had given someone and so it'd been saved; everything else was lost when their house caught fire when their greenhouse burned.

When we returned to the living room Polly said, "You're as methodical as you were as a child." Yes, she was probably right: I'd put my books on shelves grouped just like I had them in Nicolet City. "You always walked on sidewalks and never took shortcuts on the grass. Where'd you get your dining set?"

"I wanted a big table and found it from a newspaper ad when Cal and I first moved back to Nicolet City." A few of the ebony and rosewood marquetry squares had been lost but otherwise the matching mahogany sideboard, hutch, table and chairs looked the same. Then I recalled a dream: I was sitting at a dining table deciding what to do. I was to be married to a local boy but couldn't go through with it. Everyone belonged to the same church or were relatives and I wanted my freedom—they thought I was mentally unstable and doomed. I felt tempted to go ahead with marriage to one I didn't love to fit in but remembered in *Brave New World*, "Orthodoxy means not thinking—not needing to think."

"It's super. And I love your grandfather clock. Does it chime?"

I nodded and said, "I'm glad you got my address. I've often thought about you. Tell me about your kids," and then wondered why women automatically asked each other first about their children.

Polly began pulling her hair through her fingers like she did as a child—if she'd been eating something sticky she'd end up with hair like Medusa. "Eddie's in Colorado. He stayed in the Air Force, never married, and loves traveling a lot. Pattee's in Wyoming and has two girls. She married a realtor and become one herself when the girls graduated from high school." She opened her purse and I knew what was coming next.

After I made my proper comments on the pictures, I said, "Your mother showed me pictures of you when I visited her but after she died I lost track of you."

"I'm glad we got in touch again. Even if it's the time in our life we're the old fogies we used to make fun of."

I laughed and said, "Hey, we're not old yet! But, I admit the last time I got towels I picked bright striped ones and realized my days of buying beige towels were over."

"Remember those days at Girl Scout camp? We had…." But I was remembering last night's dream of going through many mazes with others at girls' camp. We were told to follow each other in two rows through long tunnels and I was terrified when the tunnel got very narrow and drew me in like a vacuum.

After Polly adjusted her slipper socks, she said, "My mother wrote me she couldn't believe your uncle or husband didn't give you any help raising your kids after your divorce."

I stared at the red crickets on her slipper socks and said, "I often think of your mother." I'd longed to tell Aunt Ida about Uncle Walt and wondered how much Polly's mother had guessed. I looked at Polly adding sugar to her tea and didn't think it'd do any good to tell her I'd been only a few hundred dollars from being eligible for food stamps after giving up my job at White Feather so I wouldn't lose custody of Mark and Jenny. I'd never lost that deep cold fear of Cal taking them away like he said if I couldn't support them.

To make Polly change topics, I told her, "I hope it doesn't snow when you're on the road."

"The forecast is for three inches tonight."

"I'd love to have you stay."

"Thanks, but I can't." Polly twisted her back again a few more times till she "hear her bones speak." The creaking never bothered me but I know it did others. "How old were Jenny and Mark when Cal died?" Polly wasn't going to let Cal go away.

"In their early twenties."

"Do you have a picture of him?"

"I found one unpacking a box before the funeral. Just a minute." When I re-entered the room with a framed black and white picture, Polly quickly flipped over her tea saucer. Had she checked my silver too? Mary Elizabeth was the one who'd always done things like that after blowing back any hair back escaping her coils. Funny, whenever I couldn't do simple things like getting the wrap off Wendy's crackers or splattering half & half getting it out of McDonald's containers, I remembered how inadequate she'd made me feel that I hadn't attended her all-girl college. Well, my silver and china were respectable even though I'd given Jenny my Wallace sterling and Lenox china I'd bought gradually over the years to have something of value to hand down. After I'd gotten the sterling and china though, I no longer admired them in Barrons catalogs and missed that.

"This is Cal's graduation picture after getting his M.D. I was going to give it to the kids but forgot to take it with me to the funeral." Cal's hair was carefully in place—he must have already been using "A little Dab'll do ya!" Brylcreem.

Polly said, "He was nice looking."

During the sixties (the decade of JFK's "Ask not what your country can do for you, ask what you can do for your country") it was only the "out-of-it" females who pursued careers because "they hadn't been able to catch a man," doomed to look like the drab old woman on the card nobody wanted in the game of Old Maid.

I asked, "Did your professors call women students "twig gatherers" because they'd work until their houses were furnished?" If women weren't married by twenty-one, it was assumed there was something wrong with them or they were not attractive enough to catch a man. The more attractive and innocent you were (why buy the cow if you could get milk through the fence) the more marketable you were—that is, you'd get husbands with the most security for your kids.

Polly said, "Well, at least your kids had a father longer than you did. You were too young to remember your father when he was killed and it was so fortunate that Walt adopted you. I'll always remember Walt as a Horatio Alger-super-American-success story."

I smiled politely and offered her more pineapple wrapped in broiled bacon, wishing I'd thought of using the Corning Ware warming tray I'd gotten for Cal.

"I suppose it worked for him too since he didn't have children of his own." When I didn't reply, Polly asked, "Where's your brother?"

"In Milwaukee. It still seems like I should be going to work and I'm not sure I'm ready for retirement. Still, things were stressing me more."

"It seems like you're pretty well settled here" and added in her extra chirpy voice, " I suppose divorce must be difficult but it happened years ago."

Tea

Tea is calming word. The word coffee sounds harsh and crude, an upstart compared with it. And in truth tea has been around longer than coffee and is even part of our history because of the Boston Tea Party. There are many kinds of tea and many interesting things to know but my knowledge is limited to what I have tried and it most likely could be life pursuit like wine tasting.

The first time I had a tea out of the ordinary was at the home of one of the members of a women's group and it seemed to say: I can afford this as my husband does well—I am a loved wife, stamped as a woman with taste and secure standing in the community. Every time I see it now in supermarkets I smile and remember the impression it made. And the day when I finally bought some and put it on my shelf with much satisfaction of having arrived. Opening the individual foil tea bags on special celebrations is done slowly as it still impresses. When I gave my daughter some I was surprised she liked it because daughters aren't supposed to agree with mothers.

My mainstay is decaffeinated in a brand I ran across that is strong and satisfies: I pour boiling water over the tea bag and watch it quickly become dark amber in my large glass mug. A glass mug once cracked when pouring for some reason. Hot tea gives comfort, warmth, settles upset stomachs.

For company, I do have china and silver teapots. It is good to have them to lend respectability: (pour very hot water in empty pots and empty before pouring tea; use an infuser with loose tea.) Tea cozies and heated trays also show you're a good housekeeper who knows how to serve tea to guests. Be prepared: some may use sugar and milk.

The First Sign

of life in my new house
were two swaying spiders
on invisible silk who took
time to make my first curtains

Lunch at Aunt Heidi's

An American flag flapped outside the car dealers. It was smaller than the one Cal had installed in our yard—he'd wanted a larger one than Uncle Walt's which was surrounded at its base by deer antlers. Uncle Walt said, "When the wind blows hard your flag sounds like my .30'06 rifle;" Aunt Hester implored, "Jesus, Mary, Joseph" that it wouldn't fall on her; the kids accepted it as part of the yard; our neighbors ignored it.

What did the salesmen think about while they walked up and down the gray floor with their hands folded behind them like Gregory Peck pacing the deck in *Moby Dick*? They paced the display floor, occasionally rubbing hoods and trunks with their sleeves. When anybody entered they eyed each other so they must've had some system, but when the First Congregational Church minister entered no one rushed to claim him.

What did the new priest at St. John's, Father Leaureaux, really believe in? What he preached and what old church doctrine held were far apart; I thought he'd seen too much—like Scarlett O'Hara's father after his wife had died in *Gone With the Wind*, their mainspring had been broken.

When I got to Aunt Heidi's she served beet soup, "using everything except the rubber bands they're sold with." She never told the ingredients in her recipes but I could tell it indeed had the entire beet (leaves, skin, roots) along with milk, potatoes, sausage, salt and pepper, garlic, and vinegar. I avoided the black grains because they were often soil and not pepper. I was never sure if she saw women raising their eyebrows at each other, but if she did it apparently didn't bother her. Uncle Walt used to tell her, "I never know what the hell kind of bugs I'll find in your cooking," but her reply was, "You've had worse things." In her dining room above her table she had a huge print of Wood's *American Gothic* as if the man's upturned pitchfork was telling critical guests where to go.

Aunt Heidi said, "Bob hasn't been sleeping well at all again." She arranged some of her crossword pencils together and continued, "Lately his nightmares about his unit freeing a concentration camp have been awful. He wakes up gasping because the stench could be smelled for miles. Once he said his unit was along a river in Germany suffering many losses only to find they were fighting their own side." She'd shown me his Bronze Star and Purple Heart. Aunt Heidi patted the crossword puzzle magazines and said, "He's sleeping downstairs so he doesn't wake me but I worry about him." I could smell the insect repellent more than usual—he had to spray all the rooms before he could sleep.

I told her about Alison's brother who'd returned from Vietnam but had to go into a VA hospital because unexpected sounds sent him running from whatever building he was in. Certain smells started him screaming and his arms were usually bleeding or infected from trying to get rid of "those crawly bloody leeches."

Aunt Heidi advised telling Allison that her brother should, "drink prune juice for iron and pray." I wondered what she'd say if I told her that I'd read in *Time* that the Catholic Church regarded women as second class and few Catholics followed its doctrine? That reports abounded about priests molesting boys? That Freud had thought Moses was an Egyptian and obsessional neurosis was a caricature of a religion? She'd just probably roll her tongue against her cheeks to hide whatever she was thinking for my own good.

I went to the C & C after for tea to settle my stomach. When I was seated, a waitress came and asked, "Just one?"

"Yes."

The waitress handed her a menu and returned with a paper place mat with "Welcome" in blue cross-stitch type lettering and dull flatware rolled in a paper napkin.

When I went to the restroom I noticed a spider on the counter so let it climb on my grocery list, carried it outside, and placed it under some shrubs hoping it wouldn't crawl into the parking lot. Spiders probably didn't live very long, but who knows—maybe they experienced more in one day than people did in a lifetime—and they'd existed millions of years before man ever evolved.

The supermarket sometimes reminded me of a PBS program about a water hole in the African Kalahari. In the summer, the tourists pushed the locals out of the best parking spots, piled their carts with steaks the locals couldn't afford because of jacked up prices, and made checkouts a pain. The locals said they were lucky to get hot dogs "without being shoved aside or trampled," and those fortunate enough to have freezers filled them by Memorial Day to last till Labor Day. Uncle Walt had Aunt Hester stock up on "thick white toilet paper," and Imperial to pour into his empty Four Roses bottles. But I enjoyed seeing the tourists and tried to guess which ones had money—and suspected they were the ones who didn't have the air, "look at me you backwoods bumpkins."

After leaving the restaurant, I found my shopping cart and got a few more things. I regretted leaving but knew if I looked too much, things wouldn't be appealing the next time and I needed to have that to look forward to since it was the only supermarket in town.

On the visit before, I paced while country music singers belted songs of undying love. The last survey I made was pasta: rotini, elbows, rigatoni, bow ties, twists (they also came in colors), angel hair, fettuccine, manicotti, mostaccioli, lasagna, penne, shells (various sizes), ruffles, vermicelli—and then egg noodles and spaghetti also in various sizes. I arranged them alphabetically, compared prices and brands. Once I surveyed luncheon meats, rings of bologna, stacked hot dogs: most were a mixture of turkey, chicken, pork, beef, and chemicals. I wrote the chemicals in symbols I remembered and compared prices and brands.

Most enjoyable, however were facial tissues: row after row of boxes. Flowers were the most popular design. Ultra soft, scented, environmentally safe, strengthened, allergenic, pop-up, baby blue, petal pink, sunny yellow, classic white. I'd pick up the most comforting for closer inspection and imagine it in my perfect house just included in the latest tour of homes to raise money for the Salvation Army.

When I looked at the rainbow of scented candles with matching labels, the meadow flowers candle conjured up the spring with Boyd, the yellow citrus the fleck in one of Cal's jackets, the blue the shore I paced thinking of Dr. Schackmann, the purple with Mitchell's heather.

Across from the candles were the detergents smelling so good you knew their claims must be true. But what did "extreme clean" mean? Was "mountain fresh" better than "spring rain"? "Deep clean" better than "ultra clean" or was "advanced action" better? Many had labels radiating rainbows.

The checkout lanes always had magazines and tabloids with features like: "Get Thin with a Garlic and Vinegar Diet," "Shocker: Star Hasn't Had Sex in Two Weeks." When I was leaving I saw the woman in the lobby collecting for the Salvation Army and it was reassuring to see her there again.

On my way home, seagulls made gigantic shadows on the road like prehistoric flying reptiles in some movie and the television tower anchored by guide wires loomed like Gulliver bound by Lilliputians.

Before turning into my drive, I saw robins gorging on the fishflies I'd seen the night before milling around the streetlight. The closer they got to the light the more crowded they became—I heard they only lived a day after hatching eggs—they were also called dayflies or mayflies. Now they were piled on the road and the ones that still fluttered caught the attention of birds; cars left slippery tracks going over them and in a week there would be little trace of them.

Still, the fishflies must know what they were doing even if their order was named after the mythical Ephemerides because of their brief life—it was where ephemeral came from I learned when I looked in the encyclopedia. Some adult species lasted less than two hours although their fossils went back millions of years. The males deposited sperm over the water like crop dusters; the females deposited eggs on the water and then died.

When opening the front door, I saw a fishfly in a spider web; I removed it but it didn't try to fly away. I always thought of keeping track of their annual appearance to see how close it was to the same day because I'd always admired the way the Indians marked time by events like when salmon swam upstream to spawn.

When Young

I thought when I was older
I'd have the answers: they
would come because
questions have answers.

By middle age I thought
insight would emerge—
it was only logical.

But answers evade as if
gathering wind with
magnets.

Preparing for the Service

When we were seated at a large round table at Big Boy, Vincent slowly shook his head and said, "If Uncle Walt had died a day earlier, it would've been on the Feast of the Immaculate Conception." When Aunt Hester crossed herself with "Jesus, Mary, Joseph!" a few times, I compared the whiteness of my knuckles and blood of too closely bitten nails to the red and white Big Boy place mat, listened to the clatter of plates and tried to float away on whiffs of Belgian Waffles. "...shrine located on the gulf near...." Vincent must be talking about his latest retreat in Mexico.

As Aunt Heidi began describing her newest corn recipe, I remembered a dream of being selected Miss Wisconsin for my corn relish recipe. I looked for Cal in the crowd wanting him to be proud of me even if thinking I'd won because corn was a top product in Wisconsin. I moved slowly like a queen holding a scepter. Aunt Hester talked about the last church bazaar until Mary Elizabeth cut in describing her new kitchen cabinets. I noticed it was getting light out and longed to be in my new home in White Rapids even though I didn't like my cabinets because they didn't look like real wood. I watched a waitress with taffy color hair hugging her head like sand ridges, walk like one of her heels was missing and after reaching under a counter she gave her underwear a quick yank.

That night I dreamed I was going to die and going to my funeral at Nicolet City's old Carnegie Library and smiled at the irony of listening to my own service like Tom Sawyer. Guns were pounding like in some war.

The next morning everyone assembled to agree with Aunt Hester on a casket with a memory drawer even before the assistant director had a chance to take off his Nicolet Explorer cap (his grandson was on the local team). He had a tendency to jerk his head like one of those toys whose head was attached to a spring, making the yellow beak of his hat resemble Donald Duck's. Aunt Hester always considered him "ugly as sin" and I wondered how the phrase began—wasn't it the attractiveness of sin that drew us like the nuns said? Uncle Walt had snickered at his "big schnozzle."

Next we went to agree with her on the flowers at Floyd's Flower & Gift where the florist had bits of fern clinging to his Flowers Are Christmas sweatshirt. Bing Crosby's *White Christmas* kept playing over and over and I kept my eyes down so I wouldn't see anything wilting, trying not to think when the red roses I helped buy would begin wilting.

The next few nights before the funeral, I heard bells toll the hours through the window I'd forced open. Staring at the street light, I wondered what'd happened to Uncle Walt's blood. How much was there? Did they just slit his wrist and let it drain like oil from a car? I'd gone to high school with Harold Stedman, the mortician/funeral director. Whenever he greeted me my eyes would drop to his hands bulging with veins like divining rods for blood and when he shook hands I couldn't wait to wash in the hottest possible water. He was a cousin of Aunt Heidi's husband and wore a mustache to conceal an overbite. I wondered how much his large sad eyes (his nickname was "Sad Sack" in school) had to do with him becoming a mortician. He'd married Sally Trilling, nicknamed, "Piggy," because of her small peevish eyes framed by sparse reddish lashes. When she tucked her hair behind her ears, kids would say, "Hey, Piggy! The flies bitin'?" They'd had a brood of kids.

On the morning of the funeral, Aunt Hester's white Olds was behind the sleek black hearse in the funeral procession: then Vincent's van (dirt seemed to stick to his Toyota like lint did to his black clothes); Scott, Jenny, and I in their Chevie Blazer; Aunt Heidi; Mark and his family; Rachel and JD; Mary Elizabeth and her husband; then other relatives and friends. The ride had a dreamlike quality; a patrol car's flashing lights leading the way allowed our flag fluttering cars to ignore stoplights and signs. I wasn't sure if I was moving or things around me were—it was the same feeling in a car wash. I remembered watching a truck with a huge red and yellow cone spinning like a garish carnival ride—when it got further away it looked like a rocket headed for Cape Canaveral. Weeks later I realized it was a cement mixer. It had red and yellow triangles on it that I tried to count while trying to remember what the yellow would be called because it was the color of the crayon between the yellow and orange ones in a big box of Crayola Crayons. The wax smell rolled over me like I'd just opened a box; whenever I got new ones, I hated to use them because they looked so perfect. Friday was art class day at St. John's when we filled in the lines of pictures with primary or analogous colors.

Clocks

Clocks themselves reveal the passage of time by how they work. Sundials are probably the oldest clocks and it is interesting to think what changes technology will have on them next. There are museums and libraries dedicated to time keeping as well as organizations and associations for people interested in the topic. I've never visited the National Watch and Clock Museum in Pennsylvania or the one in Connecticut but they would be fascinating places to spend time exploring.

My first clock that I remember is my grandfather's mantle clock that I learned to tell time, and then those round black institutional ones in school. Each clock I've had seems to exude a different personality: whether it's the face, tick, alarm, hands, numbers, if it has a second hand, luminous dial, how big it is, where it came from, where I was at the time—all has to do with how we relate. With time I've become more aware of readability and for an alarm have graduated to the boom with the extra loud alarm, shaking wakeup, flashing luminous face with a battery backup in case of power failure. At the opposite end is a grandfather clock of mellow wood, brass face and pendulum, Winchester chimes, a key to wind it up to keep its steady ticking. In between the boom and the grandfather is a battery clock in a satisfying Baskerville font.

They are so much a part of one's day how our ancestors got along without them? They obviously did fine with the help of the sun and moon, the seasons, changes in what was around them. My grandfather's clock in the living room seems now a decorative piece as I don't remember him using it. There wasn't any other around nor had he a watch so time was much his own. When it got dark, my grandmother lit an oil lamp. I was more aware of the subtleties of light and other tellers of time then.

The Last Doll

She's the last doll I got for Christmas, the only one with long hair
and she sits with two other survivors grouped in conversation
in a pink dress with three shiny buttons without compare.

She has puffed sleeves, white shoes and stockings to wear
and a new place within the group in steady rotation;
she's the last doll I got for Christmas, the only one with long hair.

The doll has no name as she seemed so rare
with braided long hair that deserved much admiration
in a pink dress with three shiny buttons without compare.

Sitting with the others she rules over them with flare,
her arms extended as if receiving ovations;
she's the last doll I got for Christmas, the only one with long hair.

Still looking new, she has needed no repair
and sits very erect as fitting her station
in a pink dress with three shiny buttons without compare.

But of the survivors, she's the one I could spare
because she's not been held as often for validation;
she's the last doll I got for Christmas, the only one with long hair
in a pink dress with three shiny buttons without compare.

Sleep

None of our night's sleep is the same as each is a dive into the subconscious which is as inexhaustible and mysterious as space itself. As I've struggled with it over the years, it seems to have its own personality not devoid of humor: that is, the more one tries to fall asleep, the more it eludes—or it comes when you don't want it to.

I've never had sleep studies but have thought of it. Perhaps there's fear of finding out how complicated it is that deters: that I'll find out something that will make me afraid of closing me eyes—falling over a cliff that I won't return. There's something about it connected to death somehow, the unknown, utter finality.

Yes, I know the recommendations: following a routine, no bright lights on in bedrooms, quiet, not eating late, warm baths, hot milk, listening to tapes of rain, a favorite pillow, sleeping pills (many have been tried), hot tea, earplugs, eyeshades, exercise, eating right.

There seems a pattern but have avoided keeping a calendar in case I would keep awake because it was expected. Perhaps it has to do with being a writer: my cousin said that her mother who wrote would write in the wee hours on a typewriter and drive her husband to distraction. Maybe it is the cost of being captivated with words, the unexpected process, the surprises in writing that keeps me on edge in anticipation, hypervigilant, afraid I'll miss something worth while: that right word, that right phrase that will begin a cascade of gorgeous lines or sentences. That it will capture what I know is there just beyond reach: the proverbial brass ring. That the merry-go-round will be forgotten and arrival will make it all golden. Except that would be boring beyond belief.

Part II

Slants and Other Perspectives

Prufrock Napkins

The white 2-fold napkins dispense like tongues at Burger King
Subway's are handkerchief square with printing in lettuce green
McDonalds's 4-folds, embossed M's fluttering doves on wing
Taco Bell's 3-folds the color of refried beans
Wendy's white 3-fold with pig-tailed girl, completes his scene.

Deciding how to fold as with damask for a napkin ring,
surveying food on plastic trays as haute cuisine
are daily events making one upswing.
He smoothes paper napkins assuming them ironed things:
how could a wrinkle presume—what could that mean?

Wiping yellow fog from windows turns napkins to string
and he drives home reinforced by caffeine
remembering rooms where the women come and go
talking of Michelangelo
wondering if he's been seen.

A Three Month Visit

When the aide returned the blood pressure cuff to the drawer she banged her arm and I smiled when she muttered something: she wore a top with a yellow cow jumping over a turquoise moon that matched her scrub pants; an orange Humpty Dumpty that was purple after he fell; and two sizes of Goldilocks with bad hair days.

A medical student with pony tail and stethoscope showed a triangle, square, circle and asked me which was the triangle, then questions after relating about Jill, a stockbroker, marrying Jack and returning to work after 3 children. Still smiling the smile for the aged, she concluded: "If you spent $3 dollars, what would you have left from $50?"

The doctor entered with a breeze of efficiency, asked again where my children lived, if I lived alone or got dizzy, had chest pain, looked at my feet without socks.

He scrolled prescriptions on a screen while I compared wall posters of food groups in pyramids.

After bidding me to "Keep well" the doctor walked me to the counter for my print-out of the visit where I picked out flying Superwoman stickers from a jar—bypassing Cinderella in her pink ball dress.

Letter to God, Revised

I'd always thought by the time I got a certain age (i.e., mature) I'd understand things and write You a letter. Now I'm mature enough to know I do not understand and that it may help if I write anyway, knowing a man would have a different frame of reference. Women are closer to the earth following cycles of the moon while orbiting the sun; men still tend to ignore Copernicus and believe everything revolves around them.

Statues of goddesses with breasts so large they must've tipped forward are common in archeology and are thought to be the first human gods—early agriculture encouraging the concept of the value of fertility. Uncovered in different parts of the world, they pretty much look the same with undefined faces.

Is it true that the Clovis culture (who may have been the first human inhabitants of the New World about 13,000 years ago) was destroyed by a comet? Or was it lack of animals to eat, or climate change? How are we to interpret the beautiful passage: "Behold the fowls of the air: for they sow not, neither do they reap, nor gather into barns; yet your heavenly Father feedeth them. Are ye not much better than they?"

Still, I can question all I want but still need to form an opinion that is at best on terra incognita—a term used on maps until coastlines and inner parts of continents had been explored. And why such an odd world of mostly surface water, a round planet rotating around a boiling star with a moon also held by gravity. A moon that was once part of the earth, now leaving it inch by inch.

Why have man evolve through developing his brains (or not survive the Ice Ages) only to have them kill each other especially in Your name, other species, threaten the survival of the planet? Go into space littering trash? With so many species extinct, will those that follow do a better job?

I see You in white robes, bearded like men artists have painted You. Being human, I can but see You in my own likeness.

Best wishes,
Carol

Hallways

The word hallway brings back going back to college after retirement. The sense of pleasure of seeing so many rooms offering classes, floor after floor of students finding their way. The feeling of adventure I always had entering one and sitting down: the freedom intoxicating. The wondering, the hope of some new idea I would grasp that would become part of me; what the professor would be like. The hush when the professor entered. The beginning to take notes. Wondering if the students really knew how lucky they were to be there, if they were really listening.

On the way out, looking into rooms also letting out. A feeling of regret class was over but there was homework to be done and there would be then next class on Monday, Wednesday, Friday; or the Tuesday and Thursday schedule. The hallways would again be there for me to come and go and I didn't mind if I was the oldest student.

In winter the floors were wet from snow being carried in and it could be slippery. In summer not all rooms had air conditioning. Even then it still brought to mind Hemingway: "If you are lucky enough to have lived in Paris as a young man, then wherever you go for the rest of your life, it stays with you, for Paris is a moveable feast."

The Hearthstone Party

The invitation to the Hearthstone Party in the township
hall was in a shape of a heart with door prize names.
After bingo played with kernels of corn markers, a Jiffy
Peanut Butter pail with slips was passed around and I
won a plastic grinning Buddha sprouting spines for jewelry,
a Pepto Bismol pink. It helped during the endless bingo games

to imagine scurrying mice behind me playing games
in the wall with their family dressed in pastels as in
Beatrix Potter books I read to the kids or sitting down
at a mushroom cap table spread with woven grass. The boy
mouse wore blue overalls and the girl mouse had long pink
pink thread apron strings. I was deciding on the exact shade

of their mother's dress when a little girl bumped
the corn markers off my bingo cards but the games
were almost over anyway. Catalogs, order forms, pencil
stubs were handed out and it was announced, "The
lady having the highest order will win an Inner Circle
Prize." In my catalog I saw a man and woman in a

gondola. Under their picture was: *Escape to Spring,*
make him follow you anywhere when you wear Legend of
Romance. The woman was trailing her hand in the moonlit
water, the tuxedo man extending tea roses and the games
not yet played between them brought sudden tears I dashed
before anyone could notice, knowing Cal would surely be

sleeping when I got home. Moths were milling around
the outside light, the grass heavy with dew, one quiet
enough to hear fireflies—a silence only broken by a passing
pickup which made the silence more intense, the stars were
more full of mystery than any science fiction games
or fairy stories for the kids. I felt one with the earth

spinning under my thin sandals and peering at sky not
obscured by trees, willed answers to questions I was

afraid to form. When I got home, a program was on
about Vietnamese Buddhist monks torching themselves
and how we weren't winning in Vietnam:
the jungle made the enemy impossible to see.

I boiled tea, watched the water turn saffron amber,
smiled at my Buddha prize, and grasped my teacup tightly
feeling the earth spin under sandals still wet with dew.

The Passing Fields

There are fields I drive by every day with the greenest weeds—not many—a sprinkling early spring between the crops growing precisely rows in newly plowed ground. The weeds, a lush green, lord over the brown fields until the corn, sugar beets, or wheat grows—some of the weeds hugging the ground, others miniature Eiffel Towers.

Every spring I wonder where they come from and conclude most seeds are carried by the wind or were already in the ground last fall. Among the regular rows of crops that grow in exact distance from one another, weeds appear as if a bravado, victory over the odds—and they expected to be even more lush when crops turned dull gold and they were still reveling in their luck of not being between sidewalk cracks, lording over the groundling crops like gothic spires.

I wonder what they're called and when they began—for sure millions of years older than the crop strains. Maybe it is the chance placement of the weeds on plowed fields that gives pause—the randomness and also the knowing if the fields were not plowed each spring, trees, shrubs, grass, and other vegetation would take over and return it to what it was for millions of years before humans graduated from hunters and gatherers.

Farmers and gardeners look at weeds differently of course—weeds that whether it rains or not grow faster than what has cost them time and money to plant. Still, I cannot help but smile at their ability annually to beat even those spring harbingers, the dandelions.

A Postcard

was in my box from White Funeral Service:
PLAN AHEAD WITH PIZZA, a number
to RSVP for Noon or 6pm to learn about
types of memorials, cremation vs. coffins.

Would we solemnly sit in a circle, or rows
in light filtered by stained glass?
Would the pizza look like the photo,
be hot, come with something to drink?

It was good the card was to RESIDENT—
it discouraged being selected as a
prime candidate for the Grim Reaper.

There's Much to See

every time you pass spice shelves in stores if you just look—
arranged Allspice to Sea Salt, green Chives to Saffron shade;
there's tales worth knowing from each to fill many a book
as they stand at attention facing you always as on parade.

Arranged Allspice to Sea Salt, green Chives to Saffron shade
capped securely waiting to be opened, all properly labeled
as they stand at attention facing you always as on parade:
common table salt to spices from caravan routes fabled.

Capped securely waiting to be opened, all properly labeled
there's tales worth knowing from each to fill many a book:
common table salt to spices from caravan routes fabled
every time you pass spice shelves in stores if you just look.

Perspective

The Blind Men and the Elephant is a well known fable. In various versions of the tale, a group of blind men (or men in the dark) touch an elephant to learn what it is like. Each one feels a different part such as the side or the tusk. When they share what each saw they do not agree. The stories differ primarily in how the elephant's body parts are described, how violent the conflict becomes and how or whether the dispute among the men and their perspectives is resolved.

I often think of the tale when others don't come up with what I do in situations which I mutter and/or cuss their lack of vision. This difference in perspective is often brought out when witnesses in cop or courtroom drama tell things differently bringing up the question of eyesight by lawyers: glasses are often not worn because of vanity we learn. The state of the viewer (frightened, tired, injured) enters into perspective. And of course the viewer's past and their connection with the scene—they could be threatened or paid to see a certain way. Perhaps the accused is a long time criminal or presents themselves badly.

What we see in everyday life is often limited from seeing it so often: people become part of the furniture. When meeting strangers we quickly form opinions from little clues that automatically place them; it saves time and we are very good at it.

This is where artists come in: they see with fresh eyes and paint accordingly. What we miss they gladly show us through their technique and interpretation pushing aside the curtains clouding our vision. We listen to experts supposed to know such things: that place the Mona Lisa as crème de la crème; navigate the slippery slopes of what blobs are modern art and those that aren't.

One Becomes Conscious

of the will to live when chemo
grinds you down

It was good to be at McDonald's
and even though Big Macs didn't
taste the same the coffee did

I'd be OK: there were three
different golden arches to visit
in town with smiling placemats

Feminism Revisited

Feminism, like other isms, is almost impossible to see when in the middle of it, living it as to speak. It was something I read in the small Midwestern newspaper under the hair dryer in the early 70's. When I read the Equal Rights Amendment didn't pass, I had little understanding what that meant—the article was crowded out by longer articles about Vietnam and the Super Bowl. The women's movement in my small town was laughed down as hippie bra burners in big cities.

I've heard the terms, backlash, waves, but I'm not sure who said it or why; like in the past, it didn't seem to have anything to do with me. It was a woman who had a lot to do with the ERA not passing I believe on Christian grounds. I just watched Clarissa, that early English novel on DVD and was not surprised that it was women who held her down so Lovelace could rape her. How often have I've seen women defend their own jailers, lash out at other women trying to change things?

They say we only see through our own lenses. And our first mirrors are our parents. If we are fortunate enough to have parents supportive of forming a positive image of ourselves, we are indeed lucky. But too often, girl babies are still second class—look at what happens to them in China. As a child, my father called me John because he'd wanted a boy.

When my daughter had a second son recently, the tears were relief it wasn't a girl because it's still a man's world where war's a game like hunting. In her time I heard coaches say to boys, "You run like a bunch of girls; you throw like a little old lady."

When my daughter first went to nursery school, I was uneasy that she played with blocks instead of dolls with the other girls and made me think I hadn't done my job even though I knew she probably did because she was used to playing blocks with her brother. Should I discourage it before a nursery mother commented? A part of me liked her independence while another said she'd have an easier future if she conformed; common sense said not to make a big deal of it.

Today there are not many magazines, literary that is, to submit poems, short stories, and essays about feminism: it seems as relevant as the dodo bird. Women smile and humor me as if I were a flower child when I mention it. And I envy their oblivion. I don't know what they think of the staggering figures of rape, domestic violence, child pornography—all acts of violence against women—acts that usually go unreported because the justice system is regarded as another rape for the victim. Where rides at night are a campus service for women attending night classes. Maybe we think we have progressed because we have names like Anne Smith-Johnson? Yet I notice in girl college students today assertiveness, an assumption of being on an equal footing that's good to see. It keeps surprising me that there isn't so much a difference in clothing as before, more of a unisex look and there isn't the pressure to marry—and yet the card game of Old Maid is still around.

Well, I'm sure you've seen things but it's this head in the sand, everything's fine attitude that makes me glad I am no longer a teacher of youth. What could I tell them about honoring life when our country is accused of imitating the British Empire? When one in three women have experienced violence? When money for education is shrinking but drug dealers, professional sports figures, questionable business prospers?

Why don't women support each other and get involved with politics? When I wrote this, the U.S. Senate has 14 women out of 100 members. Is it because it is all a man's game and as women we don't know how to play? It has been hard for women to succeed in business because they tend to work cooperatively and not top down—again, a man's game set up by men's mind frame. At least recently we've become more aware of using such terms as chairperson instead of chairman.

We have come a long way from women as child bearers determining our lives—ironically, the pioneering feminist, Mary Wollstonecraft, died after childbirth.

Do women have it easier now? Often I hear women who work and have a family say that their mates leave the bulk of the housework and childcare to them. Women are often under the strain of playing Superwoman and often lose their climb up the career ladder to have children and stay home. Salaries are still higher for men and there is the traditional assumption that men are the breadwinners. It's enough to make one think that the curse of Eve is indeed live and well—I believe the reason often given why childbirth's so painful.

A Road Familiar

You can see them if not covered with snow by the sides of roads:
seasonal yellow, white, purple, blue blossoming weeds.
Tall, short, leaning towards the sun through brown of those
still standing where they once lived a season.

Spring, Summer, Fall, Winter I drive the road but leaves, rain,
snow are not the same; the face in the mirror is from several
seasons ago. The Earth is whirling, traveling around the Sun
in an universe expanding, the Moon inching each year away.

Coming after Summer, the wind in Fall is wild and to be
remembered: branches break, leaves shake, grind, strip with
abandon, twist and spin on roads until they rest. Please tell
me about the wind of Fall so I can understand.

As I Stood

a bit to the side, I saw the surface
of the high white marble altar
of my childhood church melt,
descend in wide loops
of lumpy gray without a sound—
and avoided seeing where the
transformed statues, gilded spires,
candles, carved Latin went.

Revisiting

To steady myself, I anxiously looked for things that hadn't changed, begrudging improvements while memories of when I'd been there competed with each other. The fast food restaurant was one I hadn't been to for years; it'd been remodeled.

The new ceiling lights increased a naked atmosphere but perhaps it was because the light imitation wood floor was so reflective: the dark, hospitable patterned carpeting was gone. Seeking to rest my eyes, I saw some landscape photographs that were good but the enjoyment was brief noting the frames were plastic.

The order counter was in the same spot—so were the windows, doors, which gave some sense of grounding. I looked in the direction where I'd always sat but sadly realized it was no longer mine so selected another closer to the door I'd entered because there had been no curb to climb.

Country music twanged but couldn't remember what it was before, just Christmas music that seemed to come earlier each year. The napkins were as generic as the prescription I was on the way to pick up. Voices seemed as if they was bouncing off the hard floor and the new tables that wobbled.

The traffic outside still streamed and the silent parade of the impersonal cars somehow offered comfort, assurance, took on the look of the passage of water of a countryside river—and tried to grasp once again that the water was never the same. I saw myself going back and both in my car swallowed up in the stream of summer, fall, winter, spring—a road I'd passed over half a century ago on the way to college before the freeway skirted the city.

The soft drink lids came from dispensers naming the sizes. The new self-serve soft drink machine offered a bewildering variety of choices and searched for something familiar; the ice didn't seem the same size but it could've been; cups had unfamiliar drawings of hearts. The salt packets were now trendy sea salt. Prices had gone up but the menu was pretty much the same. The catsup cups were plastic and I took it back along with the food boxes for recycling. The clock I didn't remember.

I wasn't sure I'd come again but now I knew what table was the most convenient, it would be easy—the shock of change wouldn't be so great and wouldn't need to wait standing in disbelief to get the layout by calling on a sense of place that'd been honed, finely tuned—a sixth sense much more than the sum of the other five. And for some reason I thought of threading a small quilting needle—needles hard to thread, easy to lose and not easily located again. And remembered D.H. Lawrence's, "… the spirit of place is a great reality."

When I'd gone back to my old college, I'd felt betrayed that it'd changed, and to ease my resentment went back to remembering a library ivy covered with Ionic columns instead of the new complex with computers. It was most likely better not to look at the restaurant when driving by next time even if it looked the same on the outside.

Ultima Thule

Ultima Thule was used by medieval cartographers was used to denote any distant place located beyond the borders of the known world. Listening to "My Heart" from *Samson and Delilah*, even if I couldn't understand the words (not unlike an old Latin mass), brought a descent into wonder. An awe that, once examined vanishes—and yet we have no choice but to go on pushing aside tears that blur. It is coming home, a knowing you are walking on water as a visitor—at once grateful and sad such things are as inevitable as change. A sense of being part of the immense unknown, every living thing, standing tiptoe asking no questions knowing it would never be again like this.

An Unlikely Introduction

I recall it: a poem in school
That sounded funny, had no rule
Told by second grade nun in black
Who never tolerated flack
And made it seem like April Fools.

Still it's known Edward Lear is cool
And sailing a "pea-green boat" you'll
Find yet to read in paperback…
I recall it.

"A runcible spoon" is a jewel
Although now you'd get ridicule
So best to be quiet—hold back;
Could "a Bong-Tree" make a comeback?
Nonsense: a nun's way to retool
I recall it.

Part III

Capturing Words

Life Spans and Books

Books have been around thousands of years in various forms. My first books were the Dick and Jane reading books to be carefully held with cardboard markers to protect them from fingers. It was as memorable day when the words got to be more than see Spot run; the word "suddenly" was a surprise. A word with motion to it, a grown up word to be savored. And the illustrations of "The Fox and the Grapes" and other edifying fables were pondered.

My grandfather had a hardcopy of the *Michigan Manual* and I memorized passages to see if I could: words I didn't know the meaning of but sounded grand and adult. It had a beautiful red cover. Then geography books that came my way were to be mastered by memorizing the 48 states and their capitals (Alaska and Hawaii were not added until 1959) in the fifth grade.

My aunt read aloud some of *The Wind in the Willows* and she enjoyed it so much it encouraged me to find books like that. In grade school the Laura Ingalls Wilder books were read and reread.

In high school the Sherlock Holmes stories captivated and the history books by Hendrik Willem van Loon devoured. The novel by John Galsworthy, *The Patrician*, a revelation of literary style.

By college, paperbacks began coming my way and I couldn't get enough of Bertrand Russell and others talked about in class. The college library was a place of awe where books were brought for you from the stacks after writing them down from the card catalog drawers.

When raising my children, I read those like *Richard Scarry's Busy, Busy World* and his other books so delightfully illustrated and some on manners that got the message across with humor. Each of my children got boxes of books with dated nameplates.

Now e-books are popular: there are thousands that are free online from Project Gutenberg. Online book stores can locate books with amazing speed.

The Library Visit

White Rapid's college library smelled new because it was. The atrium with spiral stairs showcasing four floors with hanging artificial vines was the focal point for photographers. A sculptor like a huge hood ornament stood at the foot of the swimming pool blue stairs.

The library couldn't enlarge by adding more floors because the structure wouldn't support it so expansion went horizontal and some student housing units were torn down. It was now round which made it difficult to know where anything once was—like the Magic Spot I'd taken the kids years ago: a log cabin built to give the illusion you were walking on walls and ceilings. It had the same low ceilings and water sprinklers as the community college at Parisburg, the same dispensers dispensing watery blue soap. Like at the high school in Parisburg, there was a watering down of thinking at the university in White Rapids—that social concept that thinking was elitist, undemocratic. Was it a lingering backlash beginning after World War I when it was assumed that the elite/educated leaders should've known better?

The elevators separating restrooms quietly whisked students to numbered floors with numbered rooms. When the first floor sliding doors opened like hungry mouths, there was the inviting scent of coffee from the lobby café.

The deserted reference area had the air of a forgotten hostess guarding shelves under ice cube tray fluorescent lights and the books gave the impression that, if they didn't have the answers, they'd done their best.

A marble top table surrounded by chairs on the top floor was worthy of a Victorian reading room; the table must've been real marble because it was too heavy to budge. The stuffed chairs (even if they didn't smell like leather) were a delight because they weren't Aunt Hester's straight backs designed to "remember your immortal soul." The carpeting on the top floor swirled mustache patterns. Sitting so her book would catch the light from the skylight, she surveyed the books on the shelves trying to decide if what they concealed was by technique, through the inadequacy of words, her own inadequacy, or if answers were just not an option. Beyond were many empty study carrels. Large round windows with nodding treetops made her wonder if she'd suddenly grown very tall like Alice.

There was a muted train whistle and she remembered a professor saying that land around railroad tracks was often the only place native growth still grew. The whistle faded like the early morning fog when she'd first heard a train whistle surrounded by tree trunks darkened with rain, leaves brilliant green, drops descending leaf to leaf—sometimes falling in a stream from cupped leaves. The rain plopping on already saturated ground gave a dull satisfying sound. Under those trees, nothing could harm her, those seven trees that'd been spared when her grandfather's land had been cleared. Louise Erdrich had noted: "We can escape gravity itself, and every semblance of geography, by moving into sheer space, and yet we cannot abandon our need for reference, identity, our pull to landscapes that mirror our most intense feelings."

A rumble of thunder returned her to earlier times before science destroyed the myth about thunder being Hendrick Hudson and his crew playing nine-pins. In a men's club chair, surrounded by knowledge arranged by the Library of Congress Classification System, she was Woman, a round peg in a square hole. No one knew her here and she wasn't sure how she felt about that; still, she had read that ancient peoples believed that if others didn't know your name they couldn't control you. Her loyalty was suspended between what she'd left and this new place.

She thought of the women in India widowed or with incapacitated husbands who had the choice of surviving by working outside the home or following tradition and starving; more than 50 percent of them believed wife beating was justified. And that in Pakistan the court demands four male witnesses if a woman is raped—if her defense isn't successful, she's ostracized. Millions of women in third world countries undergo genital mutilation as a centuries-old rite to ensure docility. Afterwards they no longer felt sexual pleasure; when one of them died no emotion was shown because the practice of mutilation wasn't even acknowledged. In Egypt, seven out of ten women agree with genital mutilation. Yet, despite risks to one's health, wasn't it more humane if one was blocked from sexual pleasure after trauma like that Hemingway soldier after World War I?

Why is our most popular fairy tale about a stepmother anxious to have her big-footed daughters marry well? Why are nursery rhymes attributed to Old Mother Goose, a kindly old woman portrayed in books like the perfect grandmotherly babysitter?

It had started to rain. Rain would make the weeds grow even faster despite the rocks a nursery had piled over plastic at her house. The ivy-like green weeds entwined deck railings and marched up the stairs to grab the doormat only to turn barbwire brown late summer when they no longer found anything to wind around.

It was easy to snag thoughts in the new library like those Native American dream catchers suspended from car mirrors. When entering, she left a part of her the way the Japanese leave shoes by the door but when ascending the swimming pool blue metal stairs she couldn't help looking where she'd smash if going over the rails. The thought brought unexplained tears and for some reason the line from the *Heart of Darkness* about Kurtz's soul: "Being alone in the wilderness, it had looked within itself, and, by Heavens! I tell you, it had gone mad."

The upper floors felt closer to the truth—perhaps height still connected with a childhood training about Heaven. Rectangular windows gave a panorama like letter boxing in some movie; if you looked at clouds long enough you were convinced again that the earth moved and could almost see falling rock particles from stars not burned up yet. If you didn't keep looking, you'd miss it all; if the day had no clouds, you could sense time by the sun. Did the ice cube fluorescent lights get brighter when the natural light faded or did it only seem like it? Looking at the passing of time made her once again try to understand collective amnesia—why history barely mentions the Spanish flu that killed 40-100 million. Yet, maybe with the World War I horrors, it'd seemed commonplace.

There was something familiar about a short man approaching with long swinging arms that was reassuring: it was that guy so often walking spring, summer, winter, and fall when she was driving. He had a peculiar rolling gait she identified with sailors on a rolling deck—or maybe it was because it was because he was barreled chested, long armed like Popeye the Sailor Man. Here, he looked like he'd escaped from an illustrated page on evolution.

The current periodical and newspaper room was where retired people (those older than herself) read foreign newspapers. The magazine shelves had a French magazine model who stared accusingly exposing a breast. Two girls with blue toenails were at the study carrels and she caught "saw him wasted," and "living on the edge." One was wearing low-slung blue shorts with "Hooters" on the back. The blond carrels had vaulted ends, which, lined up row after row, resembled pews: misguided Protestant pews since all the Catholic ones she'd known were dark.

The psychedelic out-of-the-seventies-carpet was red, purple, burnt orange—blue circles that could be suns, pink arrows that could be feathers, turquoise triangles that could be leaves. Once drawn in, it was hard getting out.

A patron's guide to the library stated how many the library could seat; that if the electronically movable shelving were arranged in a straight line it would reach from White Rapids to Waukesha. That the expansion of sixty-nine percent more square feet would serve "today, tomorrow, and beyond." She saw the shelves strung like railroad tracks in a bird's eye view and tried to understand the guide's subtitle: "Enlarging Tradition through Technology." Most of the guide was on computer hardware—numbers and letters like: 1.4 GHz, 512 MB PC800 RDRAM, 40GB 7200RPM, 3Com 10/100.

A book review of Ian Hacking's *Rewriting the Soul: Multiple Personality and the Science of Memory* said that 90% of people with multiple personalities were women—mostly sexually abused as children. That before 1972, multiple personalities were far and few between; twenty years later thousands of cases were diagnosed in the United States alone. Reviewer, Marc Rothenberg, noted: "Intellectual and social context play a large role in diagnostics; illness has been and is historically formed."

When she returned a book to the book drop resembling one for after hours banking, it gave such a clunk she muttered, "Sorry." When she'd checked it out, the student assistant had pointed both index fingers at her and made a clicking sound moving his thumbs as if pulling triggers then went to help a girl with expandable bookshelves that wouldn't expand.

The train whistle seemed more rarefied from the top floor of the library, like it'd traveled purer air. A ghostly sound which—if visible would be a pale wispy gray. It had a warning tone today, as if reminding that everything changed.

The black and white clock was unsentimental, naked, institutional—the kind in schools and hospitals only thicker because Janus-like, it looked both ways.

Coming from the direction where matted rectangular frames were precisely placed on the middle of the wall like aprons on an expansive stomach, walked a librarian leading a guided tour. The librarian looked like she knew she no longer belonged to a select group and looked uncertain, that she'd gone down the rabbit hole of technology, and like Alice, hadn't considered "how in the world she was to get out."

The new faculty looked not much older than students, unaware that they were lucky not to be teaching K-12. Students knew however, even though teachers tried to keep them in their childhood cocoon, that things were more complicated than being a safety patrol person, a cheerleader or football player—

and there were few myths now to guide them out of labyrinths.

She'd taken a chair by the window, wondering again, why the walls were a dark wine that absorbed lighting. The floor that the expanding bookshelves moved on railroad-like tracks was a bit uneven, and encouraged a wariness of being smashed when you walked between them.

Would she ever get used to seeing students on cell phones? It was bottled water they carried before like umbilical cords. How could they sleep so soundly with people milling about like that?

Did she think that libraries should still be like the Carnegie library in Nicolet City with a marble fireplace, a grandfather clock? This new library had clocks in sync with the United States atomic clocks at the military agency, the Directorate of Time.

The books in the new library had a wary look. Even old ones held their marble-look end papers and protective tissues like Victorian ladies holding their skirts against the march of time. When she saw trees beyond the window at the opposite side of the floor, it was evident that the library wasn't really that large and it was the atrium that lent the illusion of space. When she left, splotches of rain gave the sidewalk a look of camouflage.

Driving home, she smiled at the billboard: Love To Do Lunch. J.C. (Jesus Christ). Having a pen in a car allows the pleasure of capturing fleeting things: smoke of burning leaves, smashed birds with raised wings. You keep two pens on the passenger seat to forget trying to scream in last night's dreams.

The Perennial Sherlock

I was in my twenties that I wrote lines from *A Study in Scarlet* when Watson was surprised Holmes didn't know the earth revolved around the sun: that part about not filling your brain with things you'll never use.

Doyle reveals little about Holmes but we look for clues as to what makes him tick even more than clues to his cases. We first meet Holmes through Dr. Watson, back from Afghanistan, and it's in London's Criterion Bar that Stamford links Watson with Holmes as a possible person to share rooms and as they say, the rest is history—the rooms at 221B Baker Street are still maintained as if he and Watson had just stepped out.

In Doyle's stories villains are often better people than their victims. I still envy Irene Adler in *A Scandal in Bohemia* for being esteemed by Holmes as "the woman."

The reader is delighted to read: "From a drop of water," said the writer, "a logician could infer the possibility of an Atlantic or a Niagara without having seen or heard of one or the other." Lines have become famous such as those about the dog not doing anything in the night, and Holmes concluding: "That was the curious incident."

What is it about Sherlock Holmes that keeps him popular? A search on Netflix my supplier of rental DVD's, turned up several—the earliest is Basil Rathbone's portrayal in 1929. Even my computer file finder spyglass icon is called Sherlock. PBS has a new Sherlock using a cell phone and laptop.

Sir Arthur Conan Doyle no longer wanted to write about Holmes so finished him off 1893 in *The Final Problem* but outraged readers demanded his return. What would he have thought of the animated series of his work set in the 22nd century London, and of *Sherlock Hound*? Even Spielberg and Wilder have directed Sherlock Holmes films.

My vote goes to actor Jeremy Brett a temperamental, intense, Sherlock— he portrayed several of his shorter and longer works in the 1990's. My videos of him are a delight. A recent televised one (not with him) about murdered young women hasn't any resemblance to any Sir Arthur Conan Doyle's work I remember reading but were like the television series *Cold Case*, or *CSI*. A current Sherlock is the very talented Benedict Cumberbatch.

Sherlock's cap, cape, and pipe are easily recognizable symbols of the detective; Sidney Paget is the most famous illustrator of Holmes stories defining our image of him in the *Strand Magazine*. A Google search of "Sherlock Holmes" had 4,20,000 hits including such sites as: the Sherlock Holmes Museum, The Sherlock Holmes Society of London, and The Sherlock Holmes Shoppe.

The first story I read, *The Adventure of the Speckled Band,* was in a freshman high school English class. It was in my twenties I copied lines from *A Study in Scarlet* when Watson was surprised Holmes didn't know the earth revolved around the sun—that part about not filling your brain with things you'll never use.

My well-thumbed 1122 page copy, *The Complete Sherlock Holmes,* with 1930 as the latest copyright has the "In Memoriam Sherlock Holmes" essay by Christopher Morley: Doyle's work originally appeared in nine separate books.

So what does make one reread Holmes? Doyle tells us little about Holmes but as readers we look for clues to what makes him tick. We carefully judge if Dr. Watson is a reliable narrator and glean clues about the character of this ordinary doctor to tell us more about Holmes.

What is gratifying about reading Doyle's stories is the atmosphere or world he manages to convey in a few words which we become a part. The villains seeking revenge are often better people than their victims, and the glimpses into English London and country life revives when the empire played a large factor in British life as well as the world. There is the pull between staid Watson and mercurial Holmes, the varied official police reactions to Holmes; characters are sharply drawn in both the upper and lower classes. I still envy Irene Adler in *A Scandal in Bohemia* for being esteemed by Holmes as "the woman" because of her wit.

The reader is delighted to read: "From a drop of water," said the writer, "a logician could infer the possibility of an Atlantic or a Niagara without having seen or heard of one or the other." And Watson calls it "twaddle" only to learn Holmes was the writer. Their relationship as it grows based on trust and respect is fascinating to trace from story to story. Lines have become famous such as those in *Silver Blaze* about the dog not doing anything in the night, and Holmes concluding: "That was the curious incident."

Edgar Allan Poe is commonly called the father of the detective story with his 1845 *Tales* so Doyle didn't invent the genre but today a first 1890 American edition of *A Study in Scarlet* would be worth thousands. Nicolas Meyer's, *The Seven-Percent Solution,* in 1974, was said to have introduced a new generation to Sherlock Holmes.

In a Study Carrel

I sat at a study carrel far enough from the clock so I wouldn't see the impatient red minute hand as I tasted D.H. Lawrence's, "Now a book lives as long as it is unfathomed. Once it is fathomed...once it is known and its meaning is fixed or established, it is dead." In the carrel, I felt tendrils extending from my mind seeking other minds in books. My sense of smell, hearing, sight, taste, and touch sharpened in the hope of meeting minds, some occurrence of alchemy.

I was never sure which triangle marked "move" to move bookshelves. I didn't trust the detection system because it would be the worst irony to be smashed by all those books you wanted to read.

My son told me about a story he was reading in high school about a leader having the choice of making knowledge available to his subjects and choosing not to for their own good. The Human Genome Project in genetic engineering can do much to help mankind, but wasn't the Manhattan Project and the atomic bomb done with good in mind?

Dr. Bradford had said when I first returned to college a few years ago we are all involved in an odyssey, a continual process of becoming—a wise concept but disconcerting and unsettling. It's best not to remember that pair of socks of Mark's I'd kept to have something of his nearby when he left for college, that, when I'd finally taken them out, crumbled like clumps of powder laundry detergent. I saw Mark, more solemn than I'd ever seen him, walk his sister down the aisle; maybe it was his black tux that made him so pale?

What was that essay I'd read in college freshman English long ago—a book of essays that I'd written INDIVIDUALITY on the cover? I found the essay by the underlined passages and written comments. It was Albert Jay Nock's *The Disadvantages of Being Educated.* I think I remembered it because of the rebellious idea that education made a person unfit for his society: its ironic tone had appealed to a freshman. Nock deplored the fact that education had changed from being involved with intellect and character to proficiency and training for a profession: for students, "His training, in a word, bore directly upon what he could do or get, while his education bore directly on neither; it bore upon what he could become and be." I'd underlined twice the lines: "Education deprives a young person of one of his most precious possessions, the sense of cooperation with his fellows. He is like a pacifist in 1917, along in spirit—a depressing situation, and especially, almost unbearably, depressing to youth." And the now popular Iraqi War, United We Stand, phrase came to mind when I read: "Education is divisive, separatist; training induces the exhilarating sense that one is doing with others what others do and thinking the thoughts that others think."

And just as contemporary is the autobiography privately published in 1907, *The Education of Henry Adams*, when Adams commented about finding himself, "jostled of a sudden by a crowd of men who seem to him ignorant that there is a thing called ignorance; who have forgotten how to amuse themselves; who cannot even understand that they are bored."

I've gone over this when bringing up my own kids. How much of a favor was I doing them teaching them to think for themselves? Does the American Dream really jog with this? Why do I shake my head at bored students looking at a computer terminal on cell phones listening to nearby friends? Would even Marshall McLuhan, "The medium is the message" man in the Sixties be amazed now? What about my grandson? If he is so easily bored at three, what will he be at thirty? How short will commercial sound bytes be then?

Galsworthy: Novelists and Craft

As writers we wonder about others who've influenced and shaped our favorite novelist's apprenticeship and craft, want to know they've struggled and didn't spring full-grown like Athena. In my case, I'm curious who John Galsworthy read and regarded the most highly—who helped this 1932 Nobel Prize in Literature become such a widely read, prolific writer of novels, plays, essays, short stories, and poems. After *The Forsyte Saga* began airing in 1969, the series became so popular that Masterpiece Theatre was created to meet the demand for great literary adaptations. The 2002 version is now being aired again on PBS.

My own Galsworthy favorite, *The Patrician*, has been the novel I've savored since high school for its lyric beauty, how every one of its words builds an inevitability rivaling a Greek classic. Each time I read it, I learn something of style, characterization, narration, point of view, mood, tone, irony, theme, dialogue, satire, imagery: it never fails to satisfy, to bring a feeling of regret for leaving its world after the last chapter of Part II. And for weeks after find myself wondering what Miltoun, Barbara, Lady Casterley, Courtier, might be doing, sniffing the dried rose-leaves of Mrs. Benton, admiring the iron will of Miltoun's grandmother—wishing for a sequel but knowing none could match it. That to wish for any other ending would be to deny its very theme: Character is Fate. I've read his other novels several times but *The Patrician* continues to have no rival although I do wish there had been more novels written featuring that most engaging character Dinny Cherrell than just the trilogy, *End of the Chapter*.

I'd like to share going to lunch with him. One of my favorite Galsworthy characters, Miltoun, would look down at places frequented by the masses, ordinary people he defined as the mob. As an upper class Englishman who died in the 1930's, Galsworthy would perhaps be dismayed—he writes about A.B.C., Gustard's, for tea scented with orange water, cake, little mahogany tables, and the creaking of women's corset stays. His world's upper middle class, living in more than one house (hereditary) in the town and country, with secure gilt securities. His books are elegant even in arrangement: chapters use Roman numerals and are divided into parts.

His books accompany me daily in early afternoons: if without one, I feel improperly dressed. Most of the other customers sit with friends, family, so having a book and writing notes encourages an occupied-with-a-purpose look and that I am not lonely or waiting for someone, or wasting time. My places do have air conditioning though short on linen, footmen, and fine china.

Usually there are no other customers reading books but rather laptops and texting. I once saw someone just sitting, not eating, just sitting, and her lack of occupation, stillness caught the eye: part of me envied her living in the moment, another part felt she was wasting time although a lot of thinking may have been going on. Even in our sleep our minds work and dreams that do surface are evidence.

It isn't Galsworthy's essays or plays I read over and over, but his novels. To write equally realistic male and female characters, old and young, rich and poor, with such style and human understanding boggles the mind. His support of animals before animal rights is as amazing as his support of women before the women's movement. With him, I don't hear crying children, coughing elders, loud teenagers, clanking trays: time is erased with his words creating the world he makes. I've thought of ordering a photograph of him but my image of him is more real.

Sometimes instead of Galsworthy, it is paperbacks of those seeking reviews that provide glimpses of new worlds and are afterwards donated to libraries. Sometimes it is books from classes I kept to further explore wondering how I missed so much and eye the publication date with disbelief. Some are Hemingway's remarkably clean writing: there is pleasure comparing his early Nick Adams stories with others. I remember Hemingway displays in museums—the awe of seeing his handwriting and how good looking, happy he looked when he was in his twenties.

Hardback copies have pages easier to keep open but are heavier to carry; it is easy to depart with traces of food on pages so avoid prized limited editions and autographed copies. Catsup has been the main contributor to blotched pages—but if they were pages I'd written they'd be considered praise.

In his address, "Six Novelists in Profile," Galsworthy places Charles Dickens first among English novelists because of his ability to convey human nature so vividly. Looking at the novel, Galsworthy notes, "Under Jane Austen, Dickens, Balzac, Stendhal, Scott, Dumas, Thackeray and Hugo, the novel attained a certain relation of part to whole; but it was left for one of more poetic feeling and greater sensibility than any of these to perfect its proportions, and introduce the principle of selection, until there was that complete relation of part to whole which goes to the making of what we call a work of art." Galsworthy regarded Ivan Turgenev as writing "in terms of atmosphere rather than in terms of fact," his poetry less poetic than his sketches and novels. I read some of Turgenev he mentions trying to catch the poetic moods Galsworthy admired without success—then realized I'd missed the obvious: writers borrow and transform, make it into their own and in the process lies the inevitable sea change.

Of Guy de Maupassant, Galsworthy writes, "The vigour of his vision, and his thought, the economy and clarity of the expression in which he clothed them, have not yet been surpassed. Better than any other writer, he has taught us what to leave out; better than any illustrated for us Flaubert's maxim: 'Study an object till its essential difference from every other is perceived and can be rendered in words.'" Galsworthy regarded him as a supreme craftsman who hated prejudice and stupidity capable of displaying deep emotion.

Galsworthy saw Leo Tolstoi's wide canvas opposite of Turgenev's, his mind more concerned with what he wanted to convey than the manner in which he did. Style according to Galsworthy, is "the power in a writer to remove all barriers between himself and the reader—the triumph of style is the creation of intimacy," and Tolstoi the master of creating the feeling of actual life, *War and Peace* the greatest novel.

Joseph Conrad he credited with having more than other novelists with a "cosmic sense" in which fate plays the important role. Galsworthy considers him supreme in "word-painting," of folding stories over and over giving "subtlety, richness, and depth" and placing Nature first, Man second. Every time I read Conrad I cannot believe English was not his native language.

Anatole France is described by Galsworthy as having a style that was "the poetry of pure reason" and credits him with influencing modern thought, perforating "prejudice and punctured idolatry so adroitly that the ventilation holes were scarcely visible, and the victims felt draughts without knowing why."

Galsworthy observes that the novel "has always been the subject of a 'tug-of-war' between two schools of thought—the school that demands of it a revelation or criticism of life, and the school that asks of it nothing but pleasure-giving invention," but contends art must have the quality of life: "a sufficient relation of part to whole, and a sufficient flavouring of the artist's temperament. For only these elements give to a piece of work the essential novelty of a living thing."

In this essay written in 1923, Galsworthy, concludes that the novelist needs to see widely, feel deeply and "mould what he has seen or felt into that which has a new and significant life of its own." He compares the novelist with Manet equating painting with jumping into the sea without knowing how to swim.

"Four More Novelists in Profile," Galsworthy relates that he began reading Dumas when he was twenty-five when crossing the Indian Ocean and read him for the next four years. Galsworthy notes, "At his best he had no peer at sustaining the interest of a tale. He generally had a number of plots, and drove them four-in-hand at a sharp and steady pace and with a fine evenness of motion." That Dumas was mostly interested in entertaining and offered no criticism of life.

Galsworthy considers Tchehov as revealing the "very soul" of the Russian people through "intuitive knowledge of human emotions" that gives his work a spiritual form in atmosphere and mood. His characters "are either too true to life or perhaps merely too Russian to be remembered by name."

Robert Louis Stevenson is characterized by Galsworthy as living in the moment and not "the type which psychologises and worries about why and wherefores," easy to read, and superior to Dumas and Dickens "in dexterity and swiftness" and an eternally youthful romanticist.

In W.H. Hudson there was "something of primitive man, something even of the beasts and birds he loved." Galsworthy regarded *Green Mansions* as so unique that he didn't catch its beauty till reading it again ten years later. "Rima, the bird girl of the forest, embodies at once the spell of Nature, and the yearning of the human soul for that intimacy with Nature which through self-consciousness—or shall we say town-life—we have lost."

As to the future of the novel, Galsworthy concludes, "Art that can stand up above the waters of life, or that can smile apart, or that can do both, is rooted in deep and quiet things, in private and fervent feelings." Written in 1928, it is interesting to note that he saw how hard it was to "call our souls our own." And, applying his own definition that books not having "life" in them will be blown away by time, I cannot see that happening to Galsworthy.

In "Reminiscences of Conrad," Galsworthy goes back to 1893 when he first met Conrad when sailing on the *Torrens*. Conrad was the experienced chief mate of the sailing ship and was convalescing from Congo fever. Galsworthy relates Conrad read "prodigiously," and for the thirty-one years he knew him that he struggled with his health and although, "Conrad was critically accepted from the very start," it was twenty years before his work generated many sales. Galsworthy noted that Conrad wrote "with blood and tears and needed seclusion for it," that he "stared life very much in the face, and distrusted those who didn't," and credited him with having a huge memory for impressions, people, and detail.

In "Creation of Character in Literature," Galsworthy regards Shakespeare's as being first of all a poet who in character creation was more of a novelist. He notes that if he hadn't been connected with acting that he might have held Cervantes's place in realistic novelists; he regards Falstaff and Hamlet as characters created through the subconscious mind.

Galsworthy notes that Turgenev created one of his characters, Bazarov, from meeting a young doctor on the train. After the journey, Turgenev thought about what the young man's way of life must be like in a diary he kept for months until he was familiar with the character, coining the term, nihilist. The sense that this was a new type, a modern character, provided the theme for Turgenev's, *Fathers and Children*.

In a personal classic account of the creative process in "Creation of Character in Literature" Galsworthy wrote: "I sink into my morning chair, a blotter on my knee, the last words or deed of some character in ink before my eyes, a pen in my hand, a pipe in my mouth, and nothing in my head. I sit. I don't intend; I don't expect; I don't even hope. I read over the last pages. Gradually my mind seems to leave the chair, and be where my character is acting or speaking, leg raised, waiting to come down, lips opened ready to say something. Suddenly, my pen jots down a movement or remark, another, another, and goes on doing this, haltingly, perhaps, for an hour or two. When the result is read through it surprises one by seeming to come out of what went before, and by ministering to some sort of possible future. Those pages, adding tissue to character, have been supplied from the store-cupboard of the subconscious, in response to the appeal of one's conscious directive sense, and in service to the saving grace of one's theme, using that word in the widest sense. The creation of character, however untrammelled and unconscious, thus has ever the guidance of what, perhaps, may best be called 'the homing instinct.'"

So I shall continue to look with awe upon the reproduction of the handwritten first page of the manuscript of *The Patrician* I keep near my computer, marvel how few crossed out words there are in the first and beginning of the second paragraph, and try to decipher the words crossed out. Perhaps some day I'll even see some of Galsworthy's manuscripts and letters at Princeton University's Firestone Library, Harvard University's Houghton Library, or Oxford University's Bodleian Library but till then can treasure his signed books. And if stuck on a desert island, he would be my first choice to be there also.

Alice's School Visit

Alice was getting tired of watching her sister keep time with her iPod. The sun glimmered and a breeze made mountains and valleys on the river where a stick swirled in the current. She watched the stick until it became a monitor on a tripod that skimmed over the waves landing on the bank near Kitty, Alice's cat. Alice read in big block letters: "Follow Me".

Alice motioned to her sister she was going for a walk. With Kitty in her backpack she followed the monitor until it hovered over a bed of moss that became a green carpet for a room filled with round tables where students were filling out printed Promising to Change Forms. Alice noticed the room had many posters (the frames exactly matched the carpeting) of famous sports figures. She watched students fly forms into a box labeled "Student Mission Statement." A boy sang as he walked, accenting the words with chains from his belt to the tune "Here We Go Around the Vinegar Jug or "Pop Goes the Weasel"

Here we go to the Tutoring Room
The Tutoring Room, the Tutoring Room
Here we go to the Tutoring Room
Kaboom, kaboom, kaboom

Heads turned and hands waved when more students came in but since there were no empty chairs Alice left until she stopped to read a hall poster (framed also to match the carpet). A bulletin board showed the most recent test scores of schools in the area and the article concluded that the tests were not valid because the questions had changed from the year before.

Alice found the cafeteria and saw the cook (her T-shirt read One Smart Cookie) talking to a chicken and an egg. Someone dropped a tray and the food changed into letters of the alphabet grouping and regrouping printed slogans. A PowerPoint showed circles joined by lines and arrows and then circles were chasing squares, the lines the arrows, and rolled on floor.

Kitty wanted to chase them so Alice left and found herself flying soon as she was outside—and once again was on the river bank with her sister. Kitty got out of the backpack and the monitor became a bobbing stick once again in the river.

Arriving at the Aha Moment

Multi-tasking and mobile technology, efforts to save time and get more work done doesn't leave much time to let things mull over which is crucial for writers: we need time to daydream, drive without talking on phones. I've gotten many good ideas washing dishes by hand and have read others have too.

Poetry especially needs this brooding time for illusive images on the wing. I do not understand how mulling works because the mind has millions of connections and science is but on the frontier regarding how the mind works. I just know enough to respect its complexities and be open to it. For years the color of spring grass after a long rain, the brilliance of the emerald, made me want to capture it in words. Finally this spring a poem came easily and was accepted the first time I sent it out. The triolet still seems like it came from someone else when I read the hard copy issue I just received. There was something awesome, that overwhelmed connected with the mystery of renewal that I was trying to capture and struggled every spring for years until the time was right.

The more acquainted I become with writing the more I am becoming convinced that it isn't the actual time spent writing, but all the rest of the time seemingly unconnected with it—we just can't say we write 2-8 hours a day. And that when we read with envy that writers produced work in an amazingly short time, it is because they have though about, mulled it over long before a word was actually written that stayed written. *The Old Man and the Sea* was composed in a short time because Hemingway was ready for it, had lived with it, it was ripe and every word didn't need to be fought for, changed, revised. I remember being amazed years ago on how short a time he wrote it but can understand it better now. The very mysterious creative writing process reminds me of black holes made in space when stars die that scientists cannot explain: equations crumble in efforts to understand them.

It was hard to imagine how writers wrote without word processors until seeing the hand written manuscript of Nobel prize winner John Galsworthy—his first page of *The Patrician* with only a change here and there. Galsworthy related getting "the germ" of the book from a young politician's face he saw at a dinner-party: "It intrigued me profoundly, set me to sorting old impressions, and ruminating...." The book was published three years later. When words fall into place as if they are being dictated as they did in Galsworthy's case, chances are it involved ruminating. *The Patrician* was published after several novels, short stories, and plays when Galsworthy was forty-four. His handwriting marched on with few crossed out words and new ones written above them in a pen flowing with various amounts of ink—short lines of about six or seven words using his complex sentences. It was confirmed when I read his preface to *Villa Rubein and Other Stories*: "I never saw, in the flesh, either De Maupassant or Tchehov—those masters of such different methods entirely devoid of didacticism—but their work leaves on me a strangely potent sense of personality. Such subtle intermingling of seer with thing seen is the outcome only of long and intricate brooding, a process not too favoured by modern life, yet without which we achieve little but a fluent chaos of clever insignificant impressions, a kind of glorified journalism, holding much the same relation to the deeply-impregnated work of Turgenev, Hardy, and Conrad, as a film bears to a play."

Brooding can also is used to describe the sitting on eggs to keep them warm to hatch. Snatches of conversation, an image, a quotation, diary entry, an expression of someone's face, a setting, can all be tucked away until they are ready to hatch into a poem, short story, essay, novel, article, or play. We are hatchers of multiple ideas, keeping them going like jugglers until one cannot be ignored, appears full grown like Athena.

Sometimes these incubating bits appear to have no connection, will not come together. Many are not ready to be used, will not be the right ones yet so just let them sit and grow. Seemingly contradictory, opposite ideas often spark the best work. The most interesting characters are those with conflicts that tear them apart and in the process let us see ourselves. As readers we enjoy piecing clues together in a mystery. Sir Arthur Conan Doyle's stories present an atmosphere as thick as London fog in which we eagerly join glimpses in English life when the empire played a large part in British life. There is the fascinating pull between staid Watson and moody Holmes and I still envy Irene Adler in *A Scandal in Bohemia* for being esteemed by Holmes as "the woman." Lines have become famous such as the dog not doing anything in the night, and Holmes noting: "That was the curious incident." Doyle's readers can only rejoice his slow early medical practice was such that it allowed him to mull his stories into being.

The image of Native American Dream Catchers used to assure good dreams to those who sleep under them, also comes to mind. They are usually located where the light reaches it in the morning so that bad dreams caught in the webbing are destroyed. Or the volcano eruption in Iceland not long ago that happened under a glacier: the melted water accumulated till it finally broke from under the glacier. Doris Lessing who was awarded the 2007 Nobel

Prize in Literature observed: "I usually spend a very long time thinking about it. Sometimes years. You know when you are able to write it. The work goes in before you start, really. You can have variations of the pattern, but the whole book must be there." Lessing was the oldest person to receive the Nobel Prize in Literature.

It is reassuring that no matter what we write, it makes us better writers: our work is not wasted even if tossed out. Make it a habit to jot down dreams soon as you awake as they can be the raw material of a lifetime.

Writers are very fortunate that writing is always possible no matter the time of the day, how old we are, where we live, how much money we have. Some writers don't even need a room of their own. I had one writing professor who wrote with the loudest music possible drinking strong coffee in a busy campus restaurant. No matter what writing you do, don't depend entirely on your spell checker as we've all had experiences like: "Eye want to right well" going through the spell checker.

The more swings you take the greater your chances of hitting the ball—in other words, try different types of writing. Each genre will hone your writing skills in a different way, keep you from falling into a rut, and make you more aware of different aspects of those magical, illusive things called words.

Some writing may depends on your stage in life—only now I've had the courage for poetry. Poetry had always been too mysterious, an unreachable niche until I asked myself what I had to lose by trying.

Quotations provide inspiration as well as give that special touch to your writing and conversation. Copying them in your own hand or typing them is an excellent way to appreciate and acquire the unique taste of master stylists. Start your own collection and use them often. Have them on hand when you need them—the more they become a part of you, the more likely you will use them naturally.

Anaïs Nin observed, "It is the function of art to renew our perception. What we are familiar with we cease to see. The writer shakes up the familiar scene, and as if by magic, we see a new meaning in it." Eggs take time to hatch—brooding is a process that can't be hurried and fortunately, we can do several eggs at a time.

Another tip regarding time is putting your work aside before sending it out no matter how hard it is waiting. Seeing it with fresh eyes one month or better yet a year, and doing revision that you now see is needed, will determine its acceptance or rejection.

Library Passages

When we think of library beginnings we think primarily of the library of Alexandria, a major center of scholarship from the 3rd century BC until 30 BC. It is unknown exactly how many thousands of papyrus scrolls it had before it burned and is believed to have above its shelves: *The Place of the Cure of the Soul.* The knowledge that was lost forever boggles the mind.

My first experience with libraries was in the early 1950's, a Carnegie public library built in 1908, one of the 1,689 funded by Andrew Carnegie, the steel industrialist. It had a fireplace and large reading tables next to newspapers and magazines. The children's section was between large windows overlooking trees; the adult books behind the librarian's desk. It was one story that one reached by stairs that seemed so imposing. It had a feeling of stability and served as a library until 1966 when new accessibility laws resulted in a new building. The magical feeling of libraries began there while exploring the worlds in books and having them overdue was unthinkable. That I could take some home remained central to my life growing: my first research paper in high school was on Andrew Carnegie. My next library in college was imposing, ivy covered and since I attended, has had 2 or 3 new ones.

After getting a graduate degree in history, I obtained one in library science and as a library consultant I had the good fortune to visit many public libraries in the 1970's. Some of them were Carnegie libraries, some very small buildings but it was inspiring to see them all dedicated to serving their communities.

I've worked in academic, special, public, and school libraries and have edited (and continue to edit) dozens of books on librarianship. When I retired and returned to college, the new library was the first place to explore; it was soon replaced by a newer one and in the transition, the stacks were in the field house. The new library has moveable stacks with many computers and I enjoyed the top floor view of the campus below although the reference area on the first floor never failed to provide hours of enjoyment: the marbled end papers, leather bindings of old books always brought pleasure. And touching books of my own in the collection made them seem more real. Other colleges I've visited have various libraries: graduate, undergraduate, medical, music, science. State libraries hold irreplaceable history. Most of the collection of the largest library in the word, the Library of Congress, comes through copyright registration.

My old dictionary provides security by my mouse pad but usually I use the dictionary on my computer or type words in my browser. The young have embraced technology without hesitation yet I cannot but help be apprehensive about the future of libraries as preservers of learning and culture. One of my anthologies is: *Preserving Local Writers, Genealogy, Photographs, Newspapers and Related Materials* for Rowman & Littlefield. Another anthology I edited for the American Library Association is *Bringing the Arts into the Library.*

A paper trail is often the only trail. Local libraries often are the first resource. Yes, there are electronic files but what about letters and other accounts so basic to historians and biographers? How much is being lost in e-books, pdf's? There is something satisfying about the feel of books, pages, newspapers, magazines: they have a solidity, a reality. Yes, I know that information has so proliferated that the sheer quantity begs for the electronic version. Technology has made my job of book editing easier and no longer as an author do I need to type hard copies and physically ship them to publishers. Some of my books are in e-books also but I haven't gotten a reader to save my eyes for work that must be done electronically.

But I digress: this is about libraries. There's a slippery slope involved connecting them now with technology and no one knows the future of course—but we're in transition as profound as in the times of Gutenberg. I've had the privilege of seeing the transition of accessing books from the card catalog to online catalogs; magazines go from print to electronic; print encyclopedia face the fate of the dodo. Rarely do I see books carried around but do see a lot of electronic devices. The third edition of *Michigan Authors* that I edited came out in print in 1993 but became an online project of the Library of Michigan and the Michigan Association for Media in Education. One of the anthologies I am working on now is *Library Outreach to Writers and Poets: Interviews and Case Studies of Cooperation.*

Still, who will be the custodians of culture, what is worth preserving, are very important questions. Libraries have given patrons free access. Will the owners of computers take over the custodianship of culture and knowledge? Who will they be? What will be their motivation, selection? Will there be takeovers like the questionable trend in current media? At least with books by authors, magazines and newspapers by various publishers, there has been a spread, a multitude of views that libraries have preserved, made available—surely basic to decision making in a democracy.

Location and Character

We all have heard the importance of location when it comes to real estate and it certainly relates to settings: who could imagine the British television period drama, *Downton Abbey,* set anyplace else except the 5,000-acre Highclere Castle in Hampshire, England? Hercule Poirot living anyplace except in the art nouveau Whitehaven Mansion? *Psycho* anywhere except at the Bates Motel?

The films and books we remember are those that make the most of settings to support character and plot. The setting doesn't have to be buildings but involve shadows, lights on dark streets as in film noir. Sherman's March through Georgia brings the Civil War home to Scarlett O'Hara in *Gone With the Wind.* When editing the 3rd. edition of *Michigan Authors,* I became very aware of what D. H. Lawrence noted: "Every people is polarized in some locality, which is home, the homeland. Different places on the face of the earth have different vital influence, different vibration, different chemical exhalation, different polarity with different stars: call it what you like. But the spirit of place is a great reality."

As writers and poets, we are usually too much a part of our setting to be very conscious of it. Often it is only when away from it that we write of it. *Out of Africa* was written after the author returned home. Some writers prefer quiet places; others do best in the middle of chaos.

The most effective use of setting is when it is an integral part of the plot, the characters. We cannot imagine Hercule Poirot anywhere else but his desk that reflects the exactness of his carefully groomed mustache. In *Elephants Can Remember,* the figures of elephants in the background reinforce the story. His displeasure of apple cores on his friend's car seat reinforces his obsessive neatness. Have the setting of your work become so familiar that it effortlessly becomes a crucial part of what you write without thinking about it.

Character portrayal is many faceted and challenging to achieve in print or film: a majority of the best loved roles in print or film depend on how well defined characters are. It isn't experimental style, exotic setting, fast paced action, special effects, that makes enduring favorites—well developed characters do. It isn't I don't enjoy scenes of Rome, Paris, London, Vienna, but when a film relies on scenery rather than characters, they leave me wanting; I can always watch travelogues. Special effects are interesting for a while as with continual fast paced action.

We are endlessly curious about those around us: for safety, security, emotional support we depend on one another as communal creatures. We seek to understand ourselves through others but being complex, people often conceal, are blind to what they really are. The television series, *The Office*, is presented through the lens of a boss lacking in self-knowledge and people management skill which contributes much of the comedy. Characters who are unaware of important elements is a dramatic tool as old as Oedipus and Aristotle's advice on characters is still relevant.

The unfolding of personality in small amounts, the humor, irony, inconsistency, and flaws we see in icons like Hercule Poirot, Sherlock Holmes, Scarlett O'Hara are more satisfactory to the reader and viewer because instead of being told we dig them out with the glee and determination of uncovering family secrets. Their names add so much also: Scarlett O'Hara with a name like Mary Smith wouldn't be the same. Those familiar with P.G. Wodehouse agree that the distinctive names he uses adds a great deal to the character definitions. Actors like Tommy Lee Jones are famous for revealing just with their face complex emotions; writers do it through craftsmanship providing tone, subtlety, that guide readers through the layers of character like one of those sets of Russian Nesting Dolls.

Character drives plot: what the main characters tick determines what will happen. Or, as Heraclitus (544 B.C. - 483 B.C.) concludes: "A man's character is his fate".

The Standard

Looking for another book, I ran across a thin maroon one with an unmistakable air of age—the passage of time marked it as its own so brought it to my work area where it contrasted glaringly with the computer. *The Standard Book of Etiquette: What to Do, What to Wear, What to Say, What to Write* edited by Prof. Charles Morris, LL.D, is 8" x 10" book that didn't give a publisher but was entered in the Library of Congress; pagination begins with 259 and ends at 368. What did the book beginning with page 1 cover?

I automatically looked for an index but there was none although it had a Table of Contents. The marble endpapers, double column pages suited it. It didn't have any writing, markings, or tears on the heavy cream colored pages, and no foxing (those brown speckles) common in older books.

The 1901 date put it before my parents were born and the time of my grandmother with her Gibson Girl hair style, lace handkerchiefs, who spoke French at strategic times during her work as midwife. Yes, it was one I'd like to go through now I had time as a retired person. When I got it years ago at a garage sale it was a curiosity, passé, something to smile at. Now that I was beginning to be regarded as a "dear old thing" it was a book I had more tolerance even though I knew 115 years since it was published was not even a blink of an eye on an Earth going around billions of years around the Sun. A planet that only had humans (and only one species at that) for a very short time. As the years passed with me, there had been an increased speed of time as if following a new law of relativity.

So I examined the book's scope the way I learned in library school. Like a fencer before a match, there were steps one did although conscious now of having more of Emerson's transparent eyeball that was absorbent rather than reflective; of valuing the solitude he suggested even if not in the middle of uninhabited nature.

I examine the stained hard cover, compare the frayed corners, delay opening it—there was anticipation it could be an important step in the odyssey begun when seeing my shadow a toddler and knowing when I did that the world was more mysterious and complicated than what it seemed. A search for connecting the dots.

There are some (the title page said, Profusely Illustrated) black and white photographs such as a football being played without helmets, hitting a ball wearing long dresses in lawn tennis. Some treatments for chilblains include pounding the bulbs of lilies to make an ointment. Suggestions for keeping a husband and father fond of his home are included for women. Rules for attending balls, soirees, bidding guests adieu, rules for leaving visiting cards appear the most outdated but many of the other rules are common sense and in use today such as consideration of the feelings of others. And what a lot of indoor amusements (parlor games) the most recognizable being: Simon Says, Blind Man's Bluff. There are even rules for organizing a literary society. Many sample letters included: Congratulating a Gentleman Upon His Marriage; Soliciting a Loan from a Friend; A Demand for Payment of Rent. There's one from Charles Dickens as a sample of conveying pleasant wishes. The rules of introductions have not changed much except gentlemen bowing to ladies. Remedies for falling hair today certainly doesn't include steeping onions in rum for a day and applying the liquid to the scalp every two days.

The book was a delight in seeing how things change and how they stay the same—and wonder how many readers it guided. There was more than one reference to English culture and the sole drawing is a cricket field. The sections about Courtship, Marriage was of special interest because I'm watching *Grey's Anatomy* on Netflix now and the cultural divide of then and now seems vast but also suspect what went on wasn't much different.

There are many books of etiquette being sold today and am sure those reading them a century from now will have many of my same thoughts—assuming that is, books (hard cover ones) will still exist. There is something satisfying about the feel, quality and workmanship of old books: seeing etiquette books especially on shelves provides security, a grasp of changing standards.

Tornado Watch

It was when I was reading Flannery O'Connor's guiding principle, "For the near blind you must write large" in the top floor of the college library, when a tornado watch was announced: the drumbeat of an unseen distant drummer, the last to leave some campus band practice, began to acquire a native's plea to the gods. The sky was a peculiar gray and the wind was rising according to the treetops. A small butterfly fluttered by like the one I'd become to pass through the window pane at Uncle Walt's basement when I couldn't remove my body.

Where were the shelter areas? The announcer said they were posted in the printer areas, but I was too hot from walking from the parking lot and flights of stairs. I fluffed my Alice in Wonderland hair away from my neck, and wondered why the marble table was cooler against my knees. Least I thought it marble—it looked like the marble in the pictures of ancient buildings, and tried not to remember that molecular structure was mostly space.

Equally fantastic was the book review of Ian Hacking's *Rewriting the Soul: Multiple Personality and the Science of Memory* I'd left off reading yesterday. I learned that 90% of people with multiple personalities are women—mostly sexually abused as children. That before 1972, multiple personalities were far and few between; twenty years later thousands of cases were diagnosed in the United States alone. The reviewer, Marc Rothenberg, noted that "Intellectual and social context play a large role in diagnostics; illness has been and is historically formed." Yes, it was true. Post-traumatic stress disorder wasn't just something soldiers got.

The carpeting had patterns like elephant ears or floppy petals—the tweed between the patterns rust and gray. When I'd leave, I'd rub my foot like a cat leaving its scent through scent glands on their pads, reluctant to leave. The library's open space combined with the hum of circulating air and endless books never failed to transform me into Superman, the sense of flying aided by the tops of tall buildings.

The train whistle seemed more rarefied from the top floor of the library, like it'd traveled purer air. A ghostly sound, abstract, which, if visible would be wispy silver gray. It had a warning tone today, as if reminding that everything changed, that if you just looked, you saw libraries giving way to the electronic pursued by the fear of becoming obsolete. Yet it felt secure on the top floor and I recalled Isak Dinesen's remark about the high country: "Looking back," she said in *Out of Africa*, "you are struck by your feeling of having lived for a time up in the air."

The black and white clock was unsentimental, naked, institutional—
the kind in schools and hospitals only thicker because, like Janus, one looked
one-way, the other the opposite. The red minute hand went too fast.

Coming from the direction where white matted rectangular frames
were precisely placed on the middle of the wall like aprons on an expansive
stomach, came a librarian leading new faculty on a guided tour. That meant
the beginning of the fall semester: that the library would lose its club-like
privacy I'd enjoyed. The librarian looked like she knew she no longer belonged
to an select group, like priests once were—the only ones able to read in earlier
cultures: she looked in fact, uncertain, as if she was beginning to realize she
was a part of the uncharted: that she'd gone down the rabbit hole, and like
Alice, hadn't considered "how in the world she was to get out" of the hands of
software vendors.

There was one thin young woman, unsmiling, wearing her teaching
face, among the men. When she passed, she looked through me, preferring
perhaps, not to see herself sitting there when she got my age. One of the faculty
had a look similar to Uncle Walt—of an artist searching for something to
embody the whole. Uncle Walt would scrutinize with sidelong glances until he
latched upon an article of clothing to disparage whoever didn't agree with him.
And do it in such a clever way that it didn't even seem remotely vicious, so that
when you saw the person, your eyes would immediately fall on the article of
clothing he'd ridiculed.

The new faculty all looked so young, not much older than students,
unaware that they were lucky not to be teaching K-12 students about 9/11, the
War in Iraq, and the U.S. role in the U.N. Students soon knew, however, even
though we tried to keep them in their childhood cocoon, that things were more
complicated than being a safety patrol person, a cheerleader or football player.
Perhaps it would be better to tell them the truth and not have them try to make
sense of things through rock stars. Movie stars have replaced the aristocracy we
once tried to follow to catch their reflected light: Lady Di was half and half.

Yet, despite all our democratic distrust of privilege, ads flourish about
owning Jaguars and such. Vatican II (1962-1965) modernizations took the
bloom off the glamour off the nation's largest church. Did President Clinton
do us any favors by becoming one with the people by his actions in office?
President George H.W. Bush by disguising his patrician background as one of
the boys from Texas? People no longer had myths as threads out of labyrinths.

I'd taken a chair by the window since the light there was better, wondering again, why the walls were a dark wine and therefore absorbed the dim ceiling lighting. There was a tall floor lamp nearby with a shade reminiscent of hats worn in rice paddies: the bulbs were two small fluorescent rings shaped like racetracks. The cord discreetly vanished in a carpeting opening. The chair was one of those spindle-back wicker-rockers circling the table as ready for a church bizarre knitting circle or frosted glasses on a veranda. One of them had a plaque, and when I felt the raised lettering, I tried to picture Mary A. Brown as I thanked her. The blond wood and blond wicker looked good but how does one hold a book or write in a rocking chair with thin bony arms however picturesque? Still, it had the advantage of poking your back so you wouldn't fall asleep, and this encouraged ready occupancy—and besides, they made you feel special and were cooler.

The floor area that the expanding bookshelves moved on railroad-like tracks was a bit raised, uneven, hollow sounding, and lent to the uneasiness of being smashed. Wouldn't the concentration of the books make for a heavier structure of flooring to support them, thereby wiping out the savings in space? It was a surprise when a shelf moved—then a girl, a library worker, came flip-flopping in thongs pushing a shelving cart. When she left I saw her shirt was one of those with a label on the outside—whether for comfort, advertisement, or fashion I didn't know.

If she'd noticed me, would she have understood I was there because it was fun? Would she have understood Robert Frost's line, "He studied Latin like the violin/Because he liked it—that an argument!" Did they teach Frost anymore?

Would she one day wake up, even if this postfeminist world of multiculturalism, and find the world groomed for her gone as surely as Scarlett's pre-Civil War world after the South was defeated? That the bread she'd been eating as a daughter and wife had been filled with preservatives and additives to maintain the tradition that obedient, religious women were worthy of love? She was lucky to have grown up after the Women's Movement and didn't have to straddle two worlds; she wouldn't have to grasp at straws to make bricks to climb walls. Or will she? Did it anger her that Women's Fiction (Romance) was also called Chick Lit?

Still, those born after the Cold War can hardly understand how it ever came about—the tension of the Bay of Pigs, of not knowing if the world was going to be blown up right then, had faded from collective memory. I'd been in college then, afraid, far from home—and, having read Thomas Wolfe, knew I couldn't go home again. And yet she'd probably have different labyrinths; I hoped before then, she'd have had a mythology class and had gotten sturdier shoes.

To my right were computer stations. They were so popular that when I saw a student at a study carrel, I took another look to reassure myself a laptop was in sight—and often there was. When I saw students in groups, it was over a computer. I preferred seeing lone students hunched over books, heads propped by clenched fists, or chewing pencils and fingernails, willing the words inside their brain—preferably for life, or at least until the next test. They wouldn't know until they were older, that it was the discipline acquired in managing the labyrinth of teaching styles, conflicting facts, and their own turmoil, that stuck with them.

The tornado watch was announced again. Was it a canned announcement for such times?

Would I ever get over that odd feeling seeing students talking on cellphones? It used to be bottled water they carried like umbilical cords. How could they sleep on lobby benches, dead to the world like that?

When I left, splotches of rain had turned the sidewalk shades of camouflage, a labyrinth of steam.

Choice of Navigators

Polaris holds such important because the Earth's axis points at the star
Almost directly and it is also called the Pole Star, Lodestar, Cynosure,
And North Star. Chosen by navigators since early times since it's by far
 The most constant in the same northern horizon position, a point secure
All year which can't be said for brighter stars. In *Julius Caesar* we read
"I am as constant as the northern star" and in Shakespeare's other work
The guiding star is used as a symbol of constancy. You'll not be mislead
If I share that Spenser described it as a "steadfast star" and it still lurks
In the writing of modern writers. Polaris holds constant while the whole
Northern sky moves around it and can be trusted more than one of our
Compasses subject to magnetic variations. Another finding we can extol
Is it's getting brighter but is not explained by those in scientific power.
On the Alaskan Flag appears gold stars forming the familiar constellation
The Big Dipper and North Star for the most northern state in the nation.

Part IV

Conjectures

Layers

When I saw an illustration of the layers of the Earth in grade school it's an image that has never left: that most of the earth is molten red is unimaginable and unsettling. The image made me able to relate to Rutherford being afraid to get out bed and falling through the floor after discovering atoms are most empty space. "Now my own suspicion is that the Universe is not only queerer than we suppose, but queerer than we can suppose" by J.B.S. Haldane is one I often think about.

There's also the relatively new concept of tectonic plates: plates that move, float, and sometimes fracture that cause earthquakes and volcanic eruptions make the ground we walk on as well as the mountain ranges. To grasp that there's just a thin crust and upper mantle broken into plates is an amazing concept—no more than that, it's a reality. Equally mind stretching is to remember all the continents were once one and could be again.

It is little wonder I tend to remember the Earth as the globe I got in the fifth grade with comfortable pastel divisions of countries surrounded by mostly blue water: the United States neatly divided into states with capitals secured with dots between carefully denoted Canada and Mexico.

I just learned that even though most of the Earth is covered with water, that by volume, water doesn't come to that much. And another thing: our brains (about 2% of our body weight) are layers of conscious and subconscious—each pretty much unexplored territory.

Shades of Gray

Dawn arrived through tightly closed blinds: the room getting form where the ceiling ended and wall began with different shades of gray—the chair against the window acquiring shape. The vertical spindles on the bed were becoming visible— there was no mistaking another day without sleep.

Perhaps it would be good to make very hot tea or coffee, end the limbo. The lace sewed to the top sheet becomes important to grasp and you're grateful for the pen in your other hand—but how much will you be able to read? Earplugs keep it a silent film and you smile picturing Charlie Chaplin.

Shifting Continents

Our continents once one, repeatedly separate, and join anew:
Pangea the most recent supercontinent, is the best known—
without national boundaries, state lines, circles of latitude.

Surrounded by water mostly in the southern hemisphere, the mood
must have been one of solitude without any boundaries or zones:
our continents once one, repeatedly separate, and join anew:

It would've been awesome to have been high in space to view
this huge supercontinent split and come back from the unknown
without national boundaries, state lines, circles of latitude.

What would've been the color of the sky—it wouldn't have been blue;
and how deep was Panthalassa the colossal ocean all on its own?
Our continents once one, repeatedly separate, and join anew.

Maps show South American, African coasts fit together—a shoo-in
and one of the marks of continental drift, plate tectonics backbone
without national boundaries, state lines, circles of latitude.

It is predicted our continents will again combine, become one (you
probably guessed) and all boundaries of states, nations, overthrown:
our continents once one, repeatedly separate, and join anew
without national boundaries, state lines, circles of latitude.

A Matter of Chance

In spring, the seeds from maple trees swirl helicopter fashion as they fall and some days resemble an invasion of butterflies. They're on my lawn, porch, in my garage, on the road to town, and on the sidewalks, parking lots in town. Where they land depends on currents of breeze or wind. Did any of the early makers of helicopters study them like the Wright brothers studied birds? There must be others that are carried by air too as when I stopped mowing some land assorted trees, shrubs, and grass laid claim.

Our Earth is among the few of about 100 planets once orbiting the Sun that survived. It is the right distance to get right amount of sunlight; has a magnetic shield to protect it from solar rays, and many other evolutionary changes that slowly made it possible for one cell life to begin; for the human species to appear just a short time ago. Everything comes from the elements formed in the explosions of stars.

When making patchwork quilts, one never knows how the strips of material will look when sewed together: the juxtaposition of color, pattern, texture, size—no two quilts come out alike. It's never known when the power will go out but one can sew by the window or flashlight; when you can't sleep there's new pieces to cut.

We are random choices of sperm and egg: the DNA variations of each boggle the mind as does one sperm entering a particular egg leaving so many others to die. Seeing the coils of DNA it's impossible for our minds to grasp the possibilities.

And marriage. My grandmother said it was a gambling of dice—but one seldom repeats vows with that in mind.

Passage of Corn Fields

Rows of new growth march each year
in plowed ground, new green arching to sky
turning emerald, developing silk, and ears.
Driving by satisfies the mind's eye—

in plowed ground, new green arching to sky.
Gold tassels rise delicate as Gothic spires
driving by satisfies the mind's eye—
expressing as if one's desires.

Gold tassels rise delicate as Gothic spires;
corn doesn't hover but rises to explore
expressing as if one's desires
determined not to be limited but to soar.

Corn doesn't hover but rises to explore:
stalks grow taller in some fields but it could be the seed
determined not to be limited but to soar;
new hybrids are planted as trials to succeed.

Stalks grow taller in some fields but it could be the seed:
popcorn, sweet, field corn—also called maize
new hybrids are planted as trials to succeed;
it's long been worshipped by Aztecs and praised.

Popcorn, sweet, field corn—also called maize
and its part in our domestication worth remembering:
it's long been worshipped by Aztecs and praised—
the passage of corn is well worth the measuring

and its part in our domestication worth remembering.
Turning emerald, developing silk, and ears
the passage of corn is well worth the measuring:
rows of new growth march each year.

Leo

The constellation, Leo, said to look like a lion that in
    Greek myth had fur that couldn't be pierced, claws
        sharper than any sword.

The outline made of Leo seen in many books looks more
    like a tea kettle or an iron to me—giving pause
        it was a man who named it.

Tradition says the huge lion was killed by Hercules as part
    of his twelve labors which makes sense because
        I've never seen a lion in the sky.

Near the Porch Rails

New weeds bring surprise—like one with red bead-like leaves this spring
nameless yet; weeds were often used by ancestors for medicine or dye—
secure in ground In sun near the porch rails, green life brings a new zing.
Nearby, white delicate Queen Anne's Lace (Wild Carrot), stretches to sky.

Nameless yet, weeds were often used by ancestors for medicine or dye;
Calling one, Heal All, is better than Prunella vulgaris, its scientific name.
Nearby, white delicate Queen Anne's Lace (Wild Carrot) stretches to sky.
Even if families grow next to one another, they're never exactly the same.

Calling one, Heal All is better than Prunella vulgaris, its scientific name;
Mouseear Chickweed, Bull Thistle, Shepherd's Purse are common weeds.
Even if families grow next to one another, they're never exactly the same—
spring arrivals from year to year are capable of sowing many seeds.

Mouseear Chickweed, Bull Thistle, Shepherd's Purse are common weeds;
secure in ground In sun near the porch rails, green life brings a new zing;
spring arrivals from year to year are capable of sowing many seeds.
New weeds bring surprise—like one with red bead-like leaves this spring.

A Dental Visit

A tooth had been bothering me for some time and sensitive toothpaste wasn't going to be the solution. I thought it'd mean another crown or root canal, but when I saw the dentist again, she said it was a wisdom tooth that should've been removed long ago and referred me.

On the way down, I saw an animal on the road and slowed up to try and see if its guts were spread out, if it were smashed enough so I didn't have to worry about it being still alive. The worst was when there was an animal next to it the following day because it could be its mate. But before I could get close, a Green Bay county road truck picked it up with some sort of invisible scoop. I'd never seen it done before.

The receptionist had me do the paperwork. The article I selected in the waiting room in *National Geographic* was about how old the earth was and said that the age of the earth was continually being pushed back; that if you reduced the earth's four and a half billion years to a day, that one hundred thousand years old humans didn't arrive till two seconds to midnight. Wrapping your mind around that was still impossible as when I tried to in high school.

Gripping my purse on my lap holding the *National Geographic*, I told the oral surgeon, "Give me all the shots you can."

"You women and your purses. All I have is a thin wallet." Was he talking about something else because he knew no matter how much he gave wouldn't numb me?

The chair side assistant said, "My purse is full of all kinds of things." Ah— she was probably in on the conspiracy—I should've asked to be put under and just wake up when it was all over.

The masked man said, "I don't understand how you women can lug that stuff. I tell my kids to give me composite pictures of my grandkids instead of one picture for each of them."

I chuckled, and it helped wondering how many grandkids he had and if they were as healthy as mine. After another shot that I didn't feel so much he said, "You carry three pairs of glasses!"

Another chuckle helped. He must've seen I was worried but I didn't think he'd want to hear about avoiding bifocals, and it was an advantage sometimes not to see things too closely.

The chair had been raised so I didn't have to read on my back waiting to "get a fat lip." The *National Geographic* said that the oldest rock yet found on earth was over four billion years old. I could see why people were upset when

Bishop Ussher's date for the first day of creation, Sunday, October 23, 4004 B.C., no longer worked.

The slick paper produced a glare and the black background made it hard to read. I looked out the window to rest my eyes, then, afraid of seeing a stray, I stared at the ceiling wondering how wisdom teeth got their name, realizing I was whirling on a planet inwardly boiling and capped with ice at both poles.

My lip was getting fat. The old familiar prep to pain. Lately hygienists were saying, "on a woman of your age it's uncommon to have all your teeth," and here I was having a wisdom tooth out.

The article said the brighter the stars look, the nearer they are. That the universe is about thirteen billion years old. To see if my mind still worked, I figured that it took the earth eight and a half billion years to form after the universe began—not that it made it any easier to comprehend.

I read that the first forms of life four billion years ago resembled blue-green algae. That it's now thought that life began on seafloor vents in mid-ocean ridges instead of pools of water. I stared at the picture captioned: LIFE BEGINS, willing it to give up the secrets. I saw hollow tubes as if made of birch bark with red tubes growing from them by a vent, a gaping blackness—the void I dreaded falling into when things in the past resurfaced. What looked like a spider could be part of the hollow tube, and it looked like a spider I'd found in my sink last year. I put the spider in the garage and found it dead the next day.

It was too exasperating not to tell what was alive and what wasn't in the picture so I went on reading: the first great extinction on earth was caused by the oxygen from capturing energy from sunlight (photosynthesis) that killed off other life forms. I put the magazine down, remembering the inscription carved in stone over the entrance of the natural history museum: "Failure To Adapt Brings Extinction" when my marriage was crumbling. Wasn't progress made by those who ignored form? What was progress?

The word, form, brought to mind *Godey's Lady's Book*, that popular nineteenth century monthly with engravings of women with sloping shoulders, pinched waists, cupid lips, displaying only tips of tiny feet. The poems, stories extolling the woman's role as wife, mother, or daughter, and the self-effacing Christian life, with illustrations of caged birds and guardian angels, was edited by Louis A. Godey.

I shook my head, took up reading again: in the Late Precambrian there were two giant continents; during the late Cenozoic, primates abandoned trees and humans developed within the last ten million years; that unlike other forms of life, humans are of the same species, and that every person is a part of the past, present, and the future; at Peru's Pyramid of the Moon, the Moche people practiced human sacrifice. When I looked at pictures of ribs with gashes (thought to indicate they took the flesh off victims), I wondered if it'd been a woman skinned when alive.

The next article was about a game preserve where some elephants approaching a herd of antelopes. The elephant matriarch unlatched the enclosure gate with her trunk and stood aside to let the antelopes escape. There wasn't a picture of the old matriarch but I imagined her eyes full of compassion. I was blinking back tears when the oral surgeon returned.

"You'll only feel a little tug," the masked man said leaning over. It helped picturing him as Zorro or the Lone Ranger with his grandkids.

It was all over in a few seconds; gauze was stuffed where the tooth had been.

"That's it? I asked."

"Yes. You must've expected it to crumble."

After a deep sigh of relief, I said, "That's really great!" After a moment I looked around and requested, "I'd like to keep the tooth if I could."

It was put in a little white envelope like the one I'd brought my x-ray: it just seemed a shame to leave it behind after all these years.

"Just stay there a minute for some postoperative instructions."

It was over! After all that worry, waiting, and hoping the ache would go away. I was grinning as much as I could with the gauze in my mouth when a girl came in to tell me to keep applying a little pressure with my teeth on the moistened gauze for fifteen minutes. She gave me a prescription for pain medication but warned me I'd feel like a couch potato when I did. I shook my head but she gave it to me anyway.

A few days later I looked at the tooth. It was bigger than I thought and shaped like a curved candy corn—only it was tipped with metal and was white except for the blood. I moved it with a piece of paper: funny, after being a part of me, I didn't want to touch it. In vain did I look for the nerves with a magnifying glass, those thread-like things causing so much pain, wondering if they'd all come out or if they died in the gaping hole. How long would it take to fill that hole looming in my mouth like that seafloor vent in the *National Geographic*? Part of me wished the tooth were still there because it'd been a part of me for so long. I scooped the tooth back into the blood-specked envelope and put it on a corner shelf.

A Time for Everything

When going to a doctor's appointment to hear the results of a test retake in June, white puffs I'd never seen before drifted like snow and I wondered what seeds they were. Kids were hanging out at the corner of Long's Funeral Home—some on bikes, some leaning against utility poles.

I made a note of the location of the only place in town selling Lady Godiva. If the news was bad, I'd buy loads of candy but not look at the flowers for fear I'd see some wilting. Better yet—have the boxes delivered—money wouldn't matter any longer nor would calories or tooth decay: day after day of the best nut assortment chocolates in gold boxes that when empty I'd pile in a graceful golden tower.

> A time to be born, and a time to die;
> a time to plant, and a time to uproot
> the plant.
> A time to kill, and a time to heal;
> a time to tear down, and a time to build.
> A time to weep, and a time to laugh;
> a time to mourn, and a time to dance.

Weren't they the words sung so often by folk singers in the Seventies? If I were to die now I'd avoid being good for nothing; I wouldn't tell Mark or Jenny because they had young children to worry about. At the end (hopefully before tiring of chocolates and videos) the doctors could shoot pain stuff in me and I'd just drift away. I had my death so pleasantly arranged down to the exact color of scented lace-edged sheets that when the doctor told me I was OK there was a definite sense of deflated drama—like a trout having a choice mayfly get away.

The Boulder

There was a boulder in my grandfather's field that I called a rock or stone when I was growing up that was too big to removed with the other stones from the field. The piled stone fences would remind me of Frost's poem about fences and neighbors when I got to college as well as Stonehenge in my history of civilization class. And in American history class if the arrow heads found near the field meant it could have been given a name by Native Americans.

As a child it meant something strange and old: that to have survived Midwest heat and cold under the open sky was worthy of respect. I would touch the pink and gray stone with wonder year after year that it was a sundial for the wind and birds. Now I believe it is made of granite from pictures I've seen for granite. And it would make sense that I now know that granite is prevalent in the Earth's crust.

It most likely was carried there by one of the Wisconsin glaciers that advanced and retreated over the Midwest as well as a large part of North America. The last of them retreated only about 11,000 years ago—the last of the glaciers. The boulder could have seen early humans and I try and picture what they looked like and if they ever thought their descendants would wonder about them. They too were travelers: their ancestors dispersing from Africa—whether by land or water is debated but probably both.

The boulder is most likely still there and it provides satisfaction to remember it even if the land belongs to a stranger now. It is hoped others will see it and wonder.

On the Passage Home

from the oncologist
shadows of birds became
flying reptiles

A TV tower held by
guide wires,
a captured Gulliver

Hemingway Under Glass

I'd seen the Hemingway in Michigan Display before
but went once more: Hemingway young, handsome,
swimming in Walloon

I sought again the letter to his friend: "Through good
fortune I escaped matrimony so why should I grumble?"
Two years later his wedding invitation near *A Moveable
Feast*

The sliding glass doors kept opening and I wondered if
any had read the line: "Idealists lead a rough life
in this world Jim"

All too soon, his tired face on the cover of *Life* near his
father's medical book and a pheasant feather

After comparing the covers of *For Whom the Bell Tol*ls,
the sliding glass opened for me

Midwestern Spring

Spring is the season that brings Midwesterners the most anticipation: the brown to green, the burst of delicate pink and white blossoms on fruit trees, the low dare devil swooping of nesting birds while driving—a welcoming confirmation that we made it through. Even dandelions delight our eyes, scattered replicas of the Sun. The first grass mowing. A celebration as new leaves cover bare limbs to make changing patterns of shade. We open the car windows driving past lilacs.

My first ritual of spring is to watch the snow piled by the plow near the garage: each day it gets smaller until only a pile of gravel remains. I am reminded of glaciers that carried boulders great distances as they shaped the Midwest leaving the Great Lakes: a blink in geological time.

Each spring I try and catch the new crocus pushing up from snow, bending to see their brave venture and smile. The first green is a hint of weeds in plowed fields that's gradually confirmed after a slow rain. I stare at the green, familiar and yet a stranger, trying to be reassured that soon grass and leaves will come. There's a shade of green that only comes in early spring that I try to absorb, and I imagine what's happening underground as the days of sun get longer. It is time to plant.

Every spring, big black ants come to my kitchen. A scout or two first and then a bunch on my counter until I discourage them by spraying a mix of vinegar and water. They move with jerks, very black and healthy, and I notice some are bigger than others; somehow they remind me of a convention of colon punctuation marks. They leave like they arrive, and I wonder where they were before and where they are going now.

Spring is the time when mowing the lawn lasts until nature claims it. When, living on a dirt road, the mud dares me to keep my car clean. When the first time the air conditioner turns on, I first see my electric bill, but the crowds of daffodils make me forget.

The Hemlock

D.H. Lawrence had noted: "Different places on the face of the earth have different vital influence, different vibration…call it what you like. But the spirit of place is a great reality." I sensed this in an old bar by the cemetery; it always looked the same—peeling paint, missing shingles on the sagging roof. A tilted sign, Whipper Will's Bar, noted the current owner who'd retained the name after his father gained renown after whipping an out-of-town customer. The whip, a relic from when it was a stagecoach stop, rested on deer antlers over the bar with an assortment of bathing beauties calendars going back to 1946.

It had been called Hemlock Bar for decades because the walls were hemlock bark. The crooked floor made sober people stumble—new comers were advised to "Grab yur drinks or they'll land there" by regulars indicating the river following US-13 out of town. The highway was the prime reason that the building was shifting—the vibration of large trucks caused the logs of the foundation to settle in the clay.

The air was always heavy with cigarette smoke and stale beer, the murky windows guarding customers from "the old ball and chain" at home. Gnarled limbs and tree stumps from the lumbering era were stacked in corners for the occassional tourist, but when one asked about the cobwebbed relics, they got outlandish answers with ill-concealed grins.

When the dim light got too dark at dusk, bulbs connected to greasy string from the high celing were pulled. The red neon BAR sign on the window was always on. It had the top loop of the letter B missing so it spelled DAR much to the disgust of Nicolet City's member of the Daughters of the American Revolution.

One of Aunt Hester's relatives had once owned it despite the fact she always denied it, calling it, "A sinful place no respectable person would be seen." And it did have a reputation. Regulars kept a space free in the parking lot for fights.

Black bears (the backfields were largely blackberry bushes) would make headlines when they wandered in through the back door. Their visits encouraged drinking because of the belief that bears "wouldn't pay attention to you when you had few," reaching the status of gospel after a picture appeared in the paper of a cub lapping beer on the counter. Drinks like "The Hair of the Bear," "Blackie's Kick" became popular and bets were placed when the next would appear.

The Hemlock Bar was in the neighborhood called the Tannery where a shoe leather-tanning mill had been that'd used local hemlock bark in the tanning process until the trees were depleted in 1923.

The Catholic cemetery was nearby. Aunt Hester headed an ongoing committee to close the bar because as soon as a burial service was finished, many men headed to the bar cussing the blackberry thorns—Uncle Walt laughed despite Aunt Hester saying the thorns were "God's way of keeping men from sin."

At funerals, *When the Saints Come Marching In*, sung off-key drifted across the field, Aunt Hester pretended she didn't hear by further compressing her lips; Uncle Walt would grin, nudge me, and say: "Damn fools, they're three sheets to the wind."

A Reflection

As years pass sleep is increasingly illusive—thoughts pile like thunderclouds, dreams bank into corners and leave one shivering in the dark expecting to be completely unraveled. Yes, President George W. Bush said we lived in uncertain times but sleep has been that way before and suspect there'll be no change after his term ends.

When I went back to college with my son not long ago, the library was no longer there and had been replaced twice. That high ceiling library was the most delightful building I'd ever been in. Its reference room had Greek statues on dark wood shelves: the men too high to see very clearly or read their names but the white busts always watched as I struggled over French, Modern Cartography, or T.S. Eliot. I can still hear the cooing of pigeons from ivy-covered eaves while waiting for books to be delivered from the stacks.

It was gratifying to see Starkweather Hall had been preserved, a copper sign denoting it as the oldest building on campus. It was old when I went up the winding stairs to buy books, its narrow twisting worn stairs creaking like something out of Agatha Christie. The stairs were only wide enough for two people so maybe that is how the flow was controlled: one going up, one going down. What would witty and urbane Nick Hornby make of a bookstore circled at night by bats?

This is supposed to be about reflection, getting back together, diving in the collective unconscious in its memory bank as old as the human race. As to when it (the collective unconscious) started, is like unwinding a ball of twine that I suspect is not unlike the Big Bang. Yet it is in this subterranean well that the best and worst of us lurks and I think writing is dipping in this well, getting our toes wet, sensing it best not to go too far or else we'll never return—or if we do, are forever changed and do not belong anymore.

From a Family History Letter

I remember Christmas in Poland—my grandmother set the table with hay under the tablecloth. Their farm consisted of several parcels of land in different places, while they lived in a village.

All the villagers had one common shepherd. He would stop at each homestead and took the cows to a grazing land. The villagers took turns to take him his noon day meal. In the evening the shepherd would stop at each home to deliver the cows, the cows seemed to know where they belonged.

My grandparents lived on a small hill, which was a sort of gathering place. There was a huge swing which all the village used. At the bottom of the hill there was a beautiful brook I used to wade in. They grew flax, spun the linen thread and made cloth on a loom. After the cloth was made, they spread it on the meadow to bleach in the sun, several times wetting it in this brook.

Epilogue

Passage

Summer ice, pleasure of the moment:
proof of time's passage—
clinking like reassuring coins
numbs your core.

Cubes round quickly,
become flat in your mouth
as glass frosts, leaving clear
trails as drops fall.

Swirling brings miniature
rings of Saturn; lifting the glass
uncovers the dreaded rings
of furniture keepers.

Evaporation could be measured
if there were days enough—
but ice has many forms.

Acknowledgments

Arriving at the Aha Moment: *The Write Room*, August 20, 2013; *Retirement and Good Living*, November 18, 2014

Chance: *Water, Earth, Air, Fire, and Picket Fences* (Lamar University Press, 2014)

Choice of Navigators: A Matter of Selection (Poetic Matrix Press, 2018)

A Dental Visit: *Glass Kite Anthology*, March 25, 2018: Issue 10

Feminism Revisited: *Salome Magazine*, January 2013

Grandmother Said: *Bellaonline.com* Fall, 2014; *Divining the Prime Meridian* (WordTech, 2015)

The Hemlock: (*Lily's Odyssey*: All Things That Matter Press, 2010)

It is Hard to Accept: *In Hubble's Shadow* (Shanti Arts, 2017)

The Last Doll: *Water, Earth, Air, Fire, and Picket Fences* (Lamar University Press, 2014); *A Matter of Selection* (Poetic Matrix Press, 2018)

The Library Visit: (*Interweavings: Creative Nonfiction*, Shanti Arts, 2017)

Midwestern Spring: *Qua Magazine* Fall 2015; (*Interweavings: Creative Nonfiction*, Shanti Arts, 2017)

Mr. Trueworthy: *Happily Never After* (Fey Publishing, June 2014)

On the Passage Home: *The William & Mary Review* Vol. 54, 2016

Passage: *Crucible* Fall, 2014; *In Hubble's Shadow* (Shanti Arts, 2017)

Passage of Corn Fields: *Contemporary Poetry*, Volume 2, Editor, Deepak Chaswal, (CreateSpace 2015)

Polly's Visit: *Lily's Odyssey* (All Things That Matter Press, 2010)

A Postcard: *Florida English Literary Journal*, 2017

Preparing for the Service: *Lily's Odyssey* (All Things That Matter Press, 2010)

Revisiting: *Thrice Fiction*, 2016

Sewing by Day: *Prisms, Particles, and Refractions* (Finishing Line Press, 2017)

The Tornado Watch: *Interweavings: Creative Nonfiction*, (Shanti Arts, 2017)

About the Writer

Carol Smallwood's over five dozen books include *Women on Poetry: Writing, Revising, Publishing and Teaching* and she's on Poets & Writers Magazine list of Best Books for Writers. Selected anthologies include: *Writing After Retirement: Tips by Successful Retired Writers* (Rowman & Littlefield, 2014); *Bringing the Arts into the Library: An Outreach Handbook* (American Library Association, 2014). *Water, Earth, Air, Fire, and Picket Fences* (Lamar University Press, 2014), *Divining the Prime Meridian* (WordTech Editions, 2015) are poetry collections; *Interweaving* and *In Hubble's Shadow* are from Shanti Arts in 2017; *Particles, and Refractions*, nominated for the Society of Midland Authors Award in Poetry); *Library Outreach to Writers and Poets* (McFarland, 2017) *In the Measuring* (Shanti Arts, 2018); *A Matter of Selection* (Poetic Matrix Press, 2018); *The Relevant Library* (McFarland, 2018); *Visits and Other Passages* (Finishing Line Press, 2018). Carol, who has founded and supports humane societies, has received multiple Pushcart Prize nominations is in such references as *Contemporary Authors Online: Biography in Context; Wikipedia.* She is a recent recipient of the Albert Nelson Marquis Lifetime Achievement Award.